Revitalizing a Nation

A Book in Two Parts

PART ONE   BELIEFS AND POLICIES
PART TWO   VISUAL EVIDENCE

REVITALIZING A NATION

A Statement of Beliefs, Opinions and Policies
Embodied in the Public Pronouncements of
GENERAL OF THE ARMY
Douglas MacArthur

Correlation and Captions by
JOHN M. PRATT

Introduction by
NORMAN VINCENT PEALE, D.D.

PUBLISHED BY
The Heritage Foundation, Inc.
75 East Wacker Drive, Chicago 1, Ill.

Distributed by GARDEN CITY BOOKS,
Garden City, New York

An Introduction

BY NORMAN VINCENT PEALE, D.D.

No MAN OF OUR TIME is more authentically the voice of real America than Douglas MacArthur. To the millions who lined the streets of our great cities to cheer and weep as he passed by, he is the personification of American tradition and history.

As he rode up great avenues 'midst vast throngs, the people through misty eyes saw in him the noble leaders of the past—Washington, Lee, Grant. And when he addressed the Congress of the United States, once again Americans heard the great truths which many, starved for them, never expected to hear again, and those who never heard them before wept unashamedly.

In this stalwart, romantic figure, the great hopes, dreams and ideals of our country come to life again. He stimulates renewed faith that the land of Washington, Jefferson and Lincoln still lives in the hearts of the people.

I shall never forget the light on General MacArthur's face and the deep feeling in his voice when he said to me "They are a wonderful people—the American people— quick, impulsive, generous, whole-hearted! You can always trust them and believe in them, for in their hearts they are good and true; in a crisis, they will do the right thing."

In the present crisis, this book outlines the sound, spiritual and practical thought of a great man who from a position of lofty eminence sees clearly the dangers facing us and gives of his rich wisdom to guide us. What he has to say reaches the spiritual side of our lives with a power found in the words of few of our leaders. Out of a lifetime experience of leadership and unsurpassed achievement, General MacArthur has gathered wisdom and insight into the great principles upon which our Republic was founded and only upon which it can endure.

This book will give you a spiritual rebirth of freedom and faith. Read it to your children so that the noble, incomparable sentences of our greatest master of English speech may fall like music upon their ears; that they, too, like yourself in your youth, may hear enunciated the immortal principles of God and country. These words will live in their hearts, and in yours, forever.

If America, land of the free, is to endure, we must rekindle on the altars of our hearts the ancient fires of faith, morality and patriotism. This book will greatly help in doing that. It should be distributed widely. It is an American document. Regardless of party affiliation, it should go into every home in America to be read, cherished and heeded.

It can, with our help, save America.

NORMAN VINCENT PEALE, D.D.

Fifth Avenue and 29th Street
New York, New York

Revitalizing a Nation

Belatedly the American people are beginning dimly to sense that, emerging from World War II, are two dynamic and irreconcilable forces striving for mastery—the free world and international Communism.

The foundation stones of this nation are the concepts and principles of the Judeo-Christian traditions and faith. Americans are free men. Their first allegiance is to their Creator—a Creator who endowed them with unalienable rights and an immortal end. Being free men it has been and is all but impossible for Americans to comprehend the basic tenets of international Communism, namely that people—human beings—are without individual entity or worth; that men are mere pawns, chattels, slaves of the State; that the State is without geographical location; that it has no national boundaries; that it encompasses the world.

During the year just past there came to this country from across the sea a man—a leader of men. He was a tall man, clear of eye, imposing in stature and lofty in mien who had met and wrestled with this "greatest scourge of mankind" and who understands fully the determining concepts and the motivating forces of international Communism. He shapes his every utterance, act and deed in consonance with this understanding. He is a man of such broad vision and knowledge that the Atlantic Ocean becomes merely a peaceful lake, although enclosed by the shores of continents, and the broad Pacific, a benign moat but on which can be carried the thriving commerce of billions of men. This man has such a knowledge of the historical past and such an insight into a divinely ordained future that he fashions the deeds of today to mesh with a tomorrow of one thousand years from now. This man is known to the world as General of the Army Douglas MacArthur.

One year ago, General of the Army Douglas Mac-Arthur was Supreme Commander of the Allied Forces in the Pacific. He is the man who on September 2, 1945, on board the battleship *Missouri* signed the instrument that made effective the unconditional surrender of Japan. On that fateful day he gave warning to the world that modern war had reached such destructiveness that it was wholly useless as a method of settling disputes between nations; that a spiritual revival was essential if the world was to be saved from destruction. He then stated: "It must be of the spirit if we are to save the flesh."

General MacArthur assumed the responsibility of re-building a nation, utterly destroyed, on the basis of "Christian purpose of helping a defeated and despairing people re-create in the East a nation." He laid the foundations for and was the architect of the Treaty of Peace with Japan.

He is the man who "held" in the south the North Korean forces, planned and executed the Inchon landing, routed and utterly defeated the armies of North Korea.

In November, 1950, the Red Chinese troops crossed the Manchurian boundary and joined forces with the scattered remnants of the North Korean army and "a new

war was an actuality." General MacArthur believed and
still believes that we had the resources at hand to defeat
this new enemy. Others thought differently or were afraid
to win . . . Time passes.

On April 12, 1951, General Douglas MacArthur, Supreme Commander of the Allied Forces in the Pacific,
was relieved of his command, stripped of all authority
and ordered to leave Japan. He was dismissed with as little consideration as though he had been a new office boy
found pilfering pennies from the cash register. Apparently it was intended that he be humiliated and that he
return disgraced.

General MacArthur had to his credit 52 years of loyal
and unquestioned service. He was a soldier. He obeyed
orders. He returned to his native land, but not as a
broken, beaten soldier. He was a "Daniel come to judgment"—with a vibrant message that thrilled, inspired
and re-created hope in the hearts of his countrymen. He
began the task of revitalizing the nation.

This volume makes no pretense of biography; no ges-
ture of narrative of the tragic incidents of the Korean
conflict; takes no sides on the violent controversy arising
from General MacArthur's belief that "once committed
to battle there is no substitute for victory." It is intended
to provide accurate, concise yet comprehensive statements, in his own words, of the beliefs, aspirations and
policies of General of the Army Douglas MacArthur.
These are recorded in Part One of this book. In Part
Two will be found the visual evidence of the warmth of
the reception tendered General MacArthur by the American people and the acceptance accorded the inspired
and dynamic message which he brought to them.

JOHN M. PRATT

Table of Contents

"animated by the sole desire to help restore, preserve and advance those great American principles and ideals of which we have been beneficiaries ourselves and are now trustees for future generations."

DOUGLAS MACARTHUR

Where I Stand

I HAVE BEEN warned by many that an outspoken course, even if it be solely of truth, will bring down upon my head ruthless retaliation—that efforts will be made to destroy public faith in the integrity of my views—not by force of just argument but by the application of the false methods of propaganda. I am told in effect that I must follow blindly the leader—keep silent—or take the bitter consequences. I had thought Abraham Lincoln had pinned down for all time this ugly code when he declared:

> "To sin by silence when they should protest makes cowards of men."

UNQUALIFIED DEDICATION I shall raise my voice as loud and as often as I believe it to be in the interest of the American people. I shall dedicate all of my energies to restoring to American life those immutable principles and ideals which your forefathers and mine handed down to us in sacred trust. I shall assist in the regaining of that moral base for both public and private life which will restore the people's faith in the integrity of public institutions and the private faith of every man in the integrity of his neighbor. I shall set my course to the end that no man need fear to speak the truth.

I could not do less, for the opportunities for service my country has given me and the honors it has conferred upon me have imposed an obligation which is not discharged by the termination of public service.

ESSENTIAL TO SURVIVAL In this day of gathering storms, as the moral deterioration of political power spreads its growing infection, it is essential that every spiritual force be mobilized to defend and preserve the religious base upon which this nation was founded. For it is that base which has been the motivating impulse to our moral and national growth. History fails to record a single precedent in which nations subject to moral decay have not passed into political and economic decline. There has been either a spiritual reawakening to overcome the moral lapse, or a progressive deterioration leading to ultimate national disaster.

Our country over many years grew prosperous and strong. We developed the spiritual resource to produce a culture and way of life based upon free individualism and rich in the essence of liberty and justice. Our commercial and agricultural progress set a pattern which early commanded universal admiration; and, through evolutionary processes, we adjusted our human relationships to enhance both the fruits of industry and the dignity of labor.

SOURCE OF STRENGTH Our great strength rests in those high-minded and patriotic Americans whose faith in God and love of country transcends all selfish and self-serving instincts. We must com-

mand their maximum effort toward a restoration to
public and private relationships of our age-old standards
of morality and ethics—a return to the religious fervor
which animated our leadership of former years to chart
a course of humility and integrity as best to serve the
public interest.

TO SAVE   On the 2nd of September 1945, just fol-
THE FLESH   lowing the surrender of the Japanese
                   Nation on the battleship MISSOURI, I
formally cautioned:

> "Men since the beginning of time have sought peace.
> Various methods through the ages have been at-
> tempted to devise an international process to pre-
> vent or settle disputes between nations. From the
> very start, workable methods were found insofar as
> individual citizens were concerned, but the mechan-
> ics of an instrumentality of larger international
> scope have never been successful. Military alliances,
> balance of power, leagues of nations, all in turn
> failed, leaving the only path to be by way of the
> crucible of war. The utter destructiveness of war
> now blots out this alternative. We have had our last
> chance. If we will not devise some greater and more
> equitable system, Armageddon will be at our door.
> The problem basically is theological and involves a
> spiritual recrudescence and improvement of human
> character that will synchronize with our almost
> matchless advances in science, art, literature, and
> all material and cultural developments of the past
> 2,000 years. It must be of the spirit if we are to save
> the flesh."

No man in the world is more anxious to avoid the
expansion of war than I. I am a one hundred per cent
disbeliever in war. The enormous sacrifices that have

been brought about by scientific methods of killing have rendered war a fantastic and impossible method for the solution of international difficulties.

MUTUAL SUICIDE — In war, as it is waged now, with the enormous losses on both sides, both will lose. I believe that the entire effort of modern society should be concentrated on an endeavor to outlaw it. This would probably take decades before it could be actually accomplished; but, you have to make a start. There is no half-way substitute.

The experience in Korea again emphasizes the utter futility of modern war—its complete failure as an arbiter of international dissensions. Its threat must be abolished if the world is to go on—and if it does not go on it will go under. We must finally come to realize that war is outmoded as an instrument of political policy, that it provides no solution for international problems; that it but threatens the participants with mutual national suicide.

We must understand that in final analysis the mounting cost of preparation for war is in many ways as materially destructive as war itself. We must find the means to avoid this great sapping of human energy and resource. This requires leadership of the highest order—a spiritual and moral leadership—a leadership which our country alone is capable of providing.

ONLY ROAD TO PEACE — While we must be prepared to meet the trial of war if war comes, we should gear our foreign and domestic policies toward the ultimate goal—the abolition of war from the face of the earth. That is what practically all mankind—all the great masses which populate the world—long and pray for. Therein lies the road, the only road, to universal peace and prosperity.

The voice of the people must be heeded.

> The implacable guide must be faith in those unchangeable principles and ideals which give spiritual strength to our Constitution.

There must be reflected that degree of humility which recognizes the religious base upon which our nation was founded, with an indomitable determination to preserve it. The threat to freedom in peace is no less sinister than in war. Our country's future must not go by default.

RELIGION AND COMMUNISM In the modern world, the evil forces of Communism seek to remove religion as the most formidable barrier to their advance. They strive to undermine public and private morals as a means of weakening and rendering indefensible areas of intended absorption. Their success serves to warn all free men of the depravity which has inevitably replaced spirituality where their dominion over peoples and races has become complete.

There are those who would have us believe that Communism embraces but the philosophy of agnosticism, rather than atheism. But this shallow pretense is easily belied by the record of ruthless and complete disregard of moral law, once Communism has seized power. Any complacent tolerance of this destructive force of evil should be replaced by an implacable and uncompromising determination to resist its every threat to basic and traditional ideals.

Human freedom always finds ostentatious vocal support from those most bent upon its suppression. It is essential, therefore, that there be assessed with cold and calculated realism the motivation of those who say much but do little. For there can be no compromise in the fight to preserve the sanctity of our religious base. We must condemn those who would corrupt the principles of individual liberty, freedom's mighty instrument of spiritual power.

ANCIENT RELIGIONS DESTROYED In many parts of the world, ancient religions have given way before the sweep of this concept of materialism which holds to the sanctity of no moral law and worships as its only god the power to suppress the Divine heritage of man. It first essays to make traitors among those of high degree and through them seeks to destroy nations and bend peoples to its malevolent will.

> Its plan is to abolish private property and free enterprise in order to secure that degree of power over material things necessary to render absolute its power to suppress the spiritual things.

It first establishes collectivism as the idealistic refuge for those who lack the will and the courage and the capacity for self-expression. This is the half-way point on the direct and undeviating road to full Communism. Thereafter, all private control over means and sources of production is abolished, and then with the political power safely in hand, this concentration of material power becomes that fearful weapon whereby every vestige of spiritual value and human freedom may be suppressed at will.

This is how it has happened before and it can happen again, unless the moral forces of a nation are sufficiently mobilized and alert to safeguard against so dreadful a threat to its cherished liberties.

SCOURGE OF MANKIND I shall continue to fight against that greatest scourge of mankind, Communism, as long as God gives me the power to fight. I shall work with you in the discharge of our common responsibilities of citizenship to the end that American policy be based upon the thoughts and needs and aspirations of the American people, unyielding to undue political pressures from abroad. I shall stand with you for an America rededicated to those sacred and inspired ideals and concepts which guided our forefathers when drawing the design of American freedom.

INTERNAL MENACE It is not of any external threat that I concern myself but rather of insidious forces working from within which have already so drastically altered the character of our free institutions —those institutions which formerly we hailed as something beyond question or challenge—those institutions we proudly called the American way of life.

Foremost of these forces is that directly, or even more frequently indirectly, allied with the scourge of imperialistic Communism. It has infiltrated into positions of public trust and responsibility—into journalism, the press, the radio and the schools. It seeks through covert manipulation of the civil power and the media of public information and education to pervert the truth, impair respect for moral values, suppress human freedom and representative government and, in the end, destroy our faith in our religious teachings.

This evil force, with neither spiritual base nor moral standard, rallies the abnormal and subnormal elements among our citizenry and applies internal pressure against all things we hold decent and all things that we hold right—the type of pressure which has caused many Christian nations abroad to fall and their own cherished freedoms to languish in the shackles of complete suppression.

Our need for patriotic fervor and religious devotion was never more impelling.

There can be no compromise with atheistic Communism—no half-way in the preservation of freedom and religion. It must be all or nothing.

SAFEGUARD OF AMERICA There are those who seek to convert us to a form of socialistic endeavor leading directly to the path of Communist slavery. As a counter-balance to those forces is the deep spiritual urge in the hearts of our people—a spiritual urge capable of arousing and directing a decisive and impelling public opinion. This, indeed, is the great safeguard and resource of America. So long as it exists we are secure for it holds us to the path of reason. It is an infallible reminder that our greatest hope and faith rests upon two mighty symbols—the Cross and the Flag; the one based upon those immutable teachings which provide the spiritual strength to persevere along the course which is just and right—the other based upon the invincible will that human freedom shall not perish from the earth. These are the mighty bulwarks against the advance of those atheistic predatory forces which seek to destroy the spirituality of the human mind and to enslave the human body.

Let us pray for the spiritual strength and innate wisdom to keep this nation to the course of freedom charted by our fathers; to preserve it as the mighty instrument on earth to bring universal order out of existing chaos; to restore liberty where liberty has perished; and to re-

establish human dignity where dignity has been suppressed.

BULWARK OF   We must unite in the high purpose
ALL FREEDOM   that the liberties etched upon the design of our life be unimpaired and
that we maintain the moral courage and spiritual leadership to preserve inviolate that mighty bulwark of all freedom, our Christian faith.

The New Japan

IN THIS postwar period of general failure to attain real peace one of the bright spots has been conquered Japan. That nation and its people long boasting of many centuries of unbroken military successes—a self-sufficient warrior race with a history of almost complete isolation from the rest of the world—at war's end was reduced largely to rubble with its people impoverished and broken in mind, body and spirit.

FAITH DESTROYED Never in history has a nation and its people been more completely crushed than were the Japanese at the end of the struggle. They had suffered more than a military debacle, more than the destruction of their armed forces, more than the elimination of their industrial bases, more even than the occupation of their land by foreign bayonets. Their entire faith in the Japanese way of life, cherished as invincible for many centuries, perished in the agony of their total defeat.

SPIRITUAL VACUUM The sudden and general destruction of Japanese institutions brought about by complete defeat left a spiritual vacuum in Japanese life to be filled either by a philosophy of good, or a philosophy of evil. Fortunately for Japan and for the free world, the country was spared the dreadful consequences of a Soviet military occupation and was brought instead within the benign guidance of the American people. Under this beneficent influence, the Japanese gradually lifted themselves from the ashes of defeat and started to build a new nation—a nation dedicated to the pursuit of new concepts and new ideals, fashioned from a blend between the best of their own ancient culture and those high precepts of ethics and morals which have been the great pillars supporting America's origin and growth.

PEOPLE WILLING   This oriental nation under the shadow of a continent plagued by the cruel misery of unending wars, pillage and natural disasters, proved willing and adept under the guiding hand of an occupation not conceived in a spirit of vengeance or mastery of victor over vanquished, but committed to the Christian purpose of helping a defeated, bewildered and despairing people recreate in the East a nation largely designed in the image of the West. New Japan was thus erected upon free institutions, somewhat similar to our own, which permitted the development of a moral base which cannot fail to favorably influence the course of events in Asia for generations to come. Discarded is the traditional intolerance of human rights, the restrictions upon human liberties, the callousness to human life, and in their place have been accepted and fused into the Japanese heart many of the Christian virtues so predominantly embodied in the American character.

A NEW CONSTITUTION   An enlightened constitution has become the great charter of Japanese liberty with enabling laws which give full effect to its immutable precepts. The Government has become truly representative of the popular will, deriving its just powers from the consent of the governed. The principle of local autonomy has been established. This permits the balance of political power to rest with the citizen at the community level and thus serves as a constant check against the excesses of centralized authority. The hated system of land tenure, so contributory to general unrest in Asia, has been abolished. Every farmer is now accorded the right and dignity of ownership of the land he long has tilled. He thus reaps the full fruits which result from his toil and labors with the incentive of free enterprise to maximize his effort to achieve increasing production. Representing over a half of Japan's total population, the agriculture workers have become an invincible barrier against the advance of socialistic ideas which would relegate all to the indignity of State servitude.

LABOR ACHIEVES DIGNITY Labor through the protection of modern laws has come into a new and heretofore unknown dignity and is making rapid strides along the course of a sound and healthy movement. The schools have been rid of the strictures upon academic freedom and public education is provided to all of the youth of the land. Universal suffrage has been established and the women of Japan have assumed their rightful role in the political life of the nation. With dignity and resolution they have brought to bear upon public affairs the morality which centers in the home and are progressively asserting a strong and healthy influence upon the course of Japan's political destiny.

COURTS OF JUSTICE The courts are proceeding in their administrative and judicial roles with universally accepted principles of justice firmly implanted in the norm of their procedure. The police have ceased to be masters and have become instead servants of the people with a decentralization in organization which permits exercise of their functions at the community, rather than national, level of government.

BUDGET BALANCED The economy of Japan has made rapid and effective advances toward the full restoration of stability and self-sufficiency and has achieved a sound basis for a frugal public administration. For the past three years, the National budget has been in complete balance with savings to permit substantial reductions in the tax load upon the people and corresponding raises in their living standard. Japan's present course in the economy of public administration follows closely the pattern sagely advised by Thomas Jefferson when he warned in speaking of our own government:

> "I place economy among the first and most important virtues and public debt as the greatest of dangers to be feared. To preserve our independence, we must not let our leaders load us with perpetual debt. We must make our choice between economy and liberty, or profusion and servitude. The same prudence which in private life would forbid our paying our money for unexplained projects, forbids it in the disposition of public money. We are endeavoring to reduce the government to the practice of rigid economy to avoid burdening the people and arming the Magistrate with a patronage of money which might be used to corrupt the principle of government."

SETTING AN EXAMPLE If Japan continues to heed this far-sighted warning and our own leaders who pretend to be disciples of the Jeffersonian teachings continue to ignore it, the time may well come when the Japanese people will be firmly established within the protective folds of our own cherished liberties, while we ourselves shall have lost them because of the assumption by our leaders of that "patronage of money" with its consequent corruption of government against which Jefferson so clearly warned. In such a tragic eventuality, we would be hard put to it indeed to answer the charge of our children and our children's children that we had recklessly squandered their rightful heritage of liberty, resource and opportunity.

THE PEACE TREATY This is but a brief outline of the new Japan which has been restored to a position of international dignity and equality under a peace treaty which, while far from flawless, embodies much of human justice and enlightenment. It is a Japan which may now assume the burden of preparing its own ground defense against predatory attack and thus in short time release our own beloved divisions for return home. With our air and naval support, Japan can with no great difficulty defend its own homeland which forms so vital a sector of the island defense system buttressing freedom and peace on the Pacific. It is a Japan in which we of the free world may find an alliance which shall merit our full faith.

SOME ALLIES FEARFUL I realize well that there are nations who fought with us to victory, while suffering grievous hurt from Japanese depredation, who understandably disagree in whole or in part.

It is hard for them to accept the realistic but tragic fact that in modern war the victor is also the loser. He suffers materially with the vanquished—oft-times more than does the vanquished. Indeed our own country in the aftermath of victory pays with a burden of accumulated debt such as to place a mortgage upon the energy and resource of many future generations. May we not hope that eventually through wise statesmanship and Christian tolerance the scars still left in war's wake may be finally healed and that the victor and vanquished, as befits the sacred cause of human freedom, will be invincibly bound together in mutual preservation.

INFLUENCE ON ASIA   Japan will reassume a position of dignity and equality within the family of nations and take a firm and invincible stand with the free world to repel those evil forces of international Communist tyranny which seek covertly or by force of arms to destroy freedom. That it may be counted upon to wield a profoundly beneficial influence over the course of events in Asia is attested by the magnificent manner in which the Japanese people have met the recent challenge of war, unrest and confusion surrounding them from the outside, and checked Communism within their own frontiers without the slightest slackening in their forward progress. I sent all four of our occupation divisions to the Korean battle front without the slightest qualms as to the effect of the resulting power vacuum upon Japan. The results fully justified my faith. I know of no nation more serene, orderly and industrious —nor in which higher hopes can be entertained for future constructive service in the advance of the human race.

The pages of history in recording America's twentieth

century contributions to human progress may, perchance, pass over lightly the wars we have fought. But, I believe they will not fail to record the influence for good upon Asia which will inevitably follow the spiritual regeneration of Japan. And this is as it should be, for construction always serves memory long after the destruction it follows is forgotten.

WAR AND   If the historian of the future should deem
PEACE   my service worthy of some slight reference,
            it would be my hope that he mention me
not as a Commander engaged in campaigns and battles, even though victorious to American arms, but rather as that one whose sacred duty it became, once the guns were silenced, to carry to the land of our vanquished foe the solace and hope and faith of Christian morals.

Could I have but a line a century hence crediting a contribution to the advance of peace, I would gladly yield every honor which has been accorded by war.

YOSHIDA WRITES
A LETTER

July 13, 1951

"General of the Army Douglas MacArthur
Waldorf Astoria Hotel
New York City
U.S.A.

"My dear General:
"The text of the Japanese Peace Treaty was made public today. I have also been informed that September 4th has been set as the date for the signing of it at San Francisco.

"On this joyful day I desire to express the profound gratitude of myself and my government to you who have long been a vigorous proponent of an early peace for Japan. It is gratifying that your efforts and exhortations have borne fruit. A fair and magnanimous treaty has been written embodying the principles as laid down first by you. I only regret I cannot see and thank you in person.

"Yours sincerely,
/s/ SHIGERU YOSHIDA."

MacARTHUR REPLIES

August 20, 1951

"His Excellency Shigeru Yoshida
Prime Minister of Japan
Tokyo, Japan

"Dear Mr. Prime Minister:

"I am delighted to have before me your thoughtful and generous note of July 13th.

"I rejoice with you and the Japanese people that a fair and just treaty is projected for early consummation. It is indeed a source of immense personal satisfaction that the spiritual and moral values which throughout have guided the formulation of Occupation policy will find permanent reflection in the instrument designed formally to restore the peace.

"Upon the political, economic and social base established so largely under your distinguished leadership, Japan's history lies before it. Continue faithful adherence to the following sound political policies and principles of good government, and healthy progress will be assured:

"Public morality is the touchstone to the people's faith in the integrity of the governmental process.

"Restraint and frugality in the use of the public purse produces economic stability, encourages individual thrift and minimizes the burden of taxation.

"Avoidance of the excessive centralization of the political power safeguards against the danger of totalitarian rule with the suppression of personal liberty, advances the concept of local autonomy and develops an acute consciousness in the individual citizen of his political responsibility. Undue paternalism in government tends to sap the creative potential and impair initiative and energy in those who thereby come to regard governmental subsidy as an inalienable right.

"The preservation, inviolate, of the economic system based upon free, private, competitive enterprise alone maximizes the initiative, the energy and in the end the productive capacity of the people.

"The vigorous and faithful implementation of the existing land laws providing land ownership for agricultural workers and of the labor laws providing industrial workers a voice in the conditions of their employment is mandatory if these all-important segments of Japanese society are to enjoy their rightful dignity and opportunity, and social unrest based upon just grievance is to be avoided.

"The Bill of Rights ordained by the Constitution must be vigilantly preserved if the government would be assured the people's full support. Public criticism should be encouraged rather than suppressed as providing a powerful check against the evils of maladministration of the political power. Freedom of speech as an inalienable right should never be challenged unless it directly violates the laws governing libel and slander.

"The courts must function as the champion of human justice and the police power be exercised with primary regard to individual rights.

"Without sacrifice of the principles of justice the devious advances of international Communism must be firmly repelled as a threat to internal peace and the national security. To such end, so long as existing international tensions exist in Asia, adequate security forces should be maintained to safeguard Japan's internal peace against any threatened external attack.

"Indeed a Japan erected firmly upon such a norm of political principle and policy, as well as setting a sure course to its own free destiny, could not fail to exercise a profound and beneficial influence upon the course of events in continental Asia. It would in addition contribute immeasurably to the spiritual and material advance of civilization.

"I have faith that the Japanese people will hold invincibly to such a course.

"Cordially yours,

/s/ DOUGLAS MacARTHUR."

YOSHIDA
TELEGRAPHS

San Francisco, California
10 September, 1951

"General of the Army Douglas MacArthur
Waldorf Astoria Hotel
New York, New York

"Peace treaty was signed the day before yesterday. My heart and the hearts of all Japanese turn to you in boundless gratitude for it is your firm and kindly hand that led us, a prostrate nation, on the road to recovery and reconstruction. It was you who first propounded the principles for a fair and generous peace which we now have at long last. In the name of the Japanese Government and people I send you our nation's heartfelt thanks.

/s/ SHIGERU YOSHIDA."

CHAPTER THREE

Asia and the Pacific

WHILE ASIA is commonly referred to as the gateway to Europe, it is no less true that Europe is the gateway to Asia, and the broad influence of the one cannot fail to have its impact upon the other.

SHACKLES
SHAKEN·

Before one may objectively assess the situation now existing there, he must comprehend something of Asia's past and the revolutionary changes which have marked her course up to the present. Long exploited by the so-called colonial powers, with little opportunity to achieve any degree of social justice, individual dignity, or a higher standard of life, such as guided our own noble administration of the Philippines, the peoples of Asia found their opportunity in the war just past to throw off the shackles of colonialism and now see the dawn of new opportunity, a heretofore unfelt dignity and the self-respect of political freedom.

Mustering half of the earth's population and 60 per cent of its natural resources, these peoples are rapidly consolidating a new force, both moral and material, with which to raise the living standard and erect adaptations of the design of modern progress to their own distinct, cultural environments. Whether one adheres to the concept of colonization or not, this is the direction of Asian progress and it may not be stopped.

MUST MEET NEW NEED In this situation it becomes vital that our own country orient its policies in consonance with this basic evolutionary condition rather than pursue a course blind to the reality that the colonial era is now past. The Asian peoples covet the right to shape their own free destiny. What they seek now is friendly guidance, understanding, and support, not imperious direction; the dignity of equality, not the shame of subjugation. Their pre-war standard of life, pitifully low, is infinitely lower now in the devastation left in war's wake. World ideologies play little part in Asian thinking and are little understood.

OBJECTIVE OF NEW ASIA What the Asian peoples strive for is the opportunity for a little more food in their stomachs, a little better clothing on their backs, a little firmer roof over their heads, and the realization of the normal nationalist urge for political freedom. These political-social conditions have but an indirect bearing upon our own national security, but form a backdrop to contemporary planning which must be thoughtfully considered if we are to avoid the pitfalls of unrealism.

OUR NEW FRONTIER To the early pioneer the Pacific coast marked the end of his courageous westerly advance—to us it should mark but the beginning. To him it delimited our western frontier—to us that frontier has been moved beyond the Pacific horizon. For we find our western defense geared to an Island chain off the coast of continental Asia from which with air and sea supremacy we can dominate any predatory move threatening the Pacific Ocean area.

Under such conditions the Pacific no longer represents menacing avenues of approach for a prospective invader —it assumes instead the friendly aspect of a peaceful lake. Our line of defense is a natural one and can be maintained with a minimum of military effort and expense. It envisions no attack against anyone nor does it provide the bastions essential for offensive operations, but properly maintained would be an invincible defense against aggression.

The holding of this littoral defense line in the western Pacific is entirely dependent upon holding all segments thereof, for any major breach of that line by an unfriendly power would render vulnerable to determined attack every other major segment. This is a military estimate as to which I have yet to find a military leader who will take exception. For that reason I have strongly recommended in the past as a matter of military urgency that under no circumstances must Formosa fall under Communist control. Such an eventuality would at once threaten the freedom of the Philippines and the loss of Japan, and might well force our western frontier back to the coasts of California, Oregon, and Washington.

ONE BILLION PEOPLE Our economic frontier now embraces the trade potentialities of Asia itself; for, with gradual rotation of the epicenter of world trade back to the Far East whence it started many centuries ago the next thousand years will find the main world problem the raising of the subnormal standard of life of its more than a billion Oriental peoples.

The opportunities for international trade then, if pursued with the vision and courage of the early pioneer will be limitless. The entire west coast well might then find its place on a parity with our eastern seaboard, each standing as a vital center of American industry with broad avenues of foreign trade and commerce immediately before it.

SURRENDER OF LEADERSHIP Such possibilities seem however beyond the comprehension of some high in our governmental circles who still feel that the Pacific coast marks the practical terminus of our advance and the westerly boundary of our immediate national interest—that any opportunity for the expansion of our foreign trade should be mainly in the area of Europe and the Middle East. Nothing could more surely put a brake upon our growth as a strong and prosperous nation. Intentionally or not, it would yield to industrialized Europe the undisputed dominion over the trade and commerce of the Far East.

More than this, it would in time surrender to European nations the moral, if not political, leadership of the Eastern Hemisphere. Nothing could more clearly attest a marked recession from that far-sighted vision which animated the pioneer of one hundred years ago.

It was the adventurous spirit of Americans which despite risks and hazards carved a great nation from an almost impenetrable wilderness; which established a pattern for modern industrialization and scientific development; which built our own almost unbelievable material progress and favorably influenced that of all others; which through the scientific advance of means of communication closed the international geographic gap to permit rapid and effective trade and commerce among the peoples of the world; which raised the living standard of the American people beyond that ever before known; and which elevated the laborer, the farmer and the tradesman to their rightful station of dignity and relative prosperity.

PIONEERING SPIRIT NEEDED It should be inconceivable that our leaders would close their eyes to any direction of opportunity—to concentrate upon any one avenue to the exclusion of any other. In the pioneering spirit, it should be our undeviating purpose to develop the maximum of global trade, ignoring only those unfriendly areas and peoples which our trade would assist in bringing abusive pressure against us.

There should be no rivalry between our east and our west—no pitting of Atlantic interests against those of the Pacific. The problem is global, not sectional. The living standard of the peoples of the Oriental East must and will be raised to a closer relativity with that of the Occidental West.

Only the Communists and their blind disciples advocate the lowering of the one to achieve a raising of the other—the Karl Marx theory of an international division of wealth to achieve a universal level.

ASIA MUST BE SERVED The course is clear. There must be such a development of opportunity that the requirements for a better life in the Oriental East may be filled from the almost unlimited industrial potential of the Occidental West. The human and material resources of the East would be used in compensation for the manufactures of the West. Once this elementary logic is recognized, trade with the Far East may be expected rapidly to expand under the stimulus of American vision, American enterprise and American pioneering spirit. The pioneer of the twentieth century has in all respects as broad an avenue of advance as did the pioneer of the nineteenth century.

In the face of such future opportunities, any concept of "scuttling" in the Pacific would be a direct negation of the spirit of our pioneer forefathers who stopped at no river, at no mountain, at no natural barrier in their driving urge to open the West. It is indulged in only by these who lack the vision to comprehend and assess the full significance of global potentialities and who lack the moral courage to take maximum advantage of them.

LIMITATION ON PROGRESS Regardless of motive, those who thus belittle our interest in the Pacific in favor of concentrating attention on the Atlantic are just as isolationist in their thinking as would be those who belittle our interest in the Atlantic in favor of concentrating on the Pacific. Either reflects a dangerously unbalanced vision. Any concept which would neglect the Pacific would not only limit our further progress as a nation and render our shores wide open to predatory attack through neglected avenues of possible enemy advance, but would yield to others our great opportunity for economic progress. It would leave our foreign trade largely centered in those who hold every competitive advantage over us. Our economic future clearly lies to the west. Availing ourselves of its full potential, our opportunity for growth is boundless—failing to do so, our economic stature would be limited to the normal domestic possibilities in local growth.

Trade with Asia has historically been largely a European monopoly, protected by colonial ties. This monopoly was broken with the demise of colonial rule at war's end and must never be restored.

THE PHILIPPINES Of our former ward, the Philippines, we can look forward in confidence that the existing unrest will be corrected and a strong and healthy nation will grow in the longer aftermath of war's terrible destructiveness. We must be patient and understanding and never fail them, as in our hour of need they did not fail us. A Christian nation, the Philippines stand as a mighty bulwark of Christianity in the Far East, and its capacity for high moral leadership in Asia is unlimited.

FORMOSA On Formosa, the Government of the Republic of China has had the opportunity to refute by action much of the malicious gossip which so undermined the strength of its leadership on the Chinese mainland. The Formosan people are receiving a just and enlightened administration with majority representation on the organs of government, and politically, economically and socially they appear to be advancing along sound and constructive lines.

THE NEW JAPAN The Japanese people since the war have undergone the greatest reformation recorded in modern history. With a commendable will, eagerness to learn, and marked capacity to understand, they have, from the ashes left in war's wake, erected in Japan an edifice dedicated to the primacy of individual liberty and personal dignity, and in the ensuing process there has been created a truly representative government committed to the advance of political morality, freedom of economic enterprise, and social justice. Politically, economically and socially Japan is now abreast of many free nations of the earth and will not again fail the universal trust.

FAITH OF OUR FATHERS If the national well being is to be served it is for us of this generation, as indeed for Americans of every generation, to assess the current strength of the pioneering spirit and appraise anew the incentives which alone can give it dynamic vitality. In so doing, it is well that we remember the composite of pioneering characteristics which have gone into the building of the great Pacific coast. Here strength overcame weakness, courage dominated fear, and the responsibility of life overshadowed the certainty of death. Here men, through an exemplification of spirituality, fashioned character as a far more meaningful and valued heritage than the material results their labors brought forth. It is that heritage of character which must be preserved by our generation so that we could do now what they did then.

We will then regain the faith of our fathers and the strength to meet the issues which perplex us now with the same determination and wisdom with which they met the issues which perplexed them then. So invincible was their faith that they inscribed upon every coin of the United States down to and including even the penny their simple profession "in God we trust." Let our faith be no less.

CHAPTER FOUR

Korea

In the Pacific we and our friends maintain an island defense chain off the coast of continental Asia which must be preserved inviolate at any cost. Despite some public statements to the contrary, there is reason to fear that it is still the over-riding purpose of some of our political leaders, under the influence of allies who maintain diplomatic ties with Communist China, to yield the Island of Formosa at an opportune time to the Chinese henchmen of international Communism. The effect of such action would be to breach our island defense chain, threaten peace on the Pacific and ultimately endanger the security of our Pacific coastal area.

There is little doubt that the yielding of Formosa and the seating of Communist China in the United Nations was fully planned when I called upon the enemy commander in Korea on March 24, 1951 to meet me in the field to arrange armistice terms. This I did in view of the fundamental weakness of his military position due to the lack of industrial base in China capable of supporting modern warfare.

OPPOSITION
LEADS
TO REPRISAL
The opposition I expressed to yielding Formosa and seating Red China, with the overwhelming support it received from the American people, unquestionably wrecked the secret plan to yield on these issues as the price for peace in Korea. There followed the violent Washington reaction in personal retaliation against me for what was actually so normal a military move.

INTEGRITY
ESSENTIAL
TO LEADERSHIP
This is an era characterized by a universal sentiment of nationalism. This we must respect if we would gain the respect of others. The peoples of the world will only follow our leadership upon the basis of our moral integrity and spiritual as well as physical strength. They will measure us not by the monies we recklessly give them, but by the general attitudes with which we face the common problems of mankind.

Possibly in Asia, where the record is more fully developed and events themselves have more plainly written the judgment, has the irresponsibility of our national policy been most pronounced. There our betrayal of China will ever stand as a black mark upon our escutcheon. But the tragedy of Korea comes closer to the hearts of the American people.

There, in the aftermath of victory in World War II, we first undertook the protection of the Korean people and the welding of their segments into a consolidated and free nation. Later we repudiated that purpose and practically invited the aggression which ensued by withdrawing our forces, enunciating the policy that the defense and consolidation of Korea was no longer within our sphere of political and military interest, and simultaneously withholding the arms needed adequately to prepare the South Korean defense force. Yet still later, after its southern half had been brought under attack from the north, we reassumed its defense and consolidation.

What is our policy in Korea?

Some will tell you that the pacification and unification of all Korea is the objective—an objective which indeed still stands as the formal mandate of the United Nations. Others tend to overlook such a formally stated policy and will tell you that our objective is achieved upon clearing South Korea of invading forces. Still others ignore both explanations and frankly say that our objective now is to continue to engage the enemy forces in Korea in a prolonged and indecisive campaign of attrition, notwithstanding the constantly increasing cost in American blood.

Who will tell you in the traditionally ringing tones of the American patriot that our objective is victory over the nation and men who, without provocation or justification, have warred against us and that our forces will be furnished all the sinews and other means essential to achieve that victory with a minimum of cost in human life?

NOT CONSULTED   While I was not consulted prior to the President's decision to intervene in support of the Republic of Korea, that decision, from a military standpoint, proved a sound one, as we hurled back the invader and decimated his forces.

We defeated the Northern Korean armies. Our victory was complete and our objectives within reach when Red China intervened with numerically superior ground forces. This created a new war and an entirely new situa-

tion—a situation not contemplated when our forces were
committed against the North Korean invaders—a situation which called for new decisions in the diplomatic
sphere to permit the realistic adjustment of military
strategy.

While no man in his right mind would advocate send-
ing our ground forces into continental China and such
was never given a thought, the new situation did urgently
demand a drastic revision of strategic planning if our
political aim was to defeat this new enemy as we had
defeated the old.

ESSENTIALS TO ENDING WAR Apart from the military need as I saw
it to neutralize the sanctuary protec-
tion given the enemy north of the
Yalu, I felt that military necessity in the conduct of the
war made mandatory—

(1) The intensification of our economic blockade
against China;
(2) The imposition of a naval blockade against the
China coast;
(3) Removal of restrictions on air reconnaissance
of China's coastal areas and of Manchuria;
(4) Removal of restrictions on the forces of the Republic of China on Formosa with logistical support to contribute to their effective operations
against the common enemy.

For entertaining these views, all professionally designed
to support our forces committed to Korea and bring hos-
tilities to an end with the least possible delay and at a
saving of countless American and Allied lives, I have
been severely criticized in lay circles, principally abroad,
despite my understanding that from a military standpoint

the above views have been fully shared in past by practically every military leader concerned with the Korean
campaign, including our own Joint Chiefs of Staff.

STALEMATE I called for reinforcements, but was in-
INDICATED formed that reinforcements were not available. I made clear that if not permitted to
destroy the enemy build-up bases north of the Yalu; if
not permitted to utilize the friendly Chinese forces of some
600,000 men on Formosa; if not permitted to blockade
the China coast to prevent the Chinese Reds from getting
succor from without; and if there were to be no hope of
major reinforcements, the position of the command from
the military standpoint forbade victory.

We could hold in Korea by constant maneuver and at
an appropriate area where our supply line advantages
were in balance with the supply line disadvantages of the
enemy, but we could hope at best for only an indecisive
campaign, with its terrible and constant attrition upon
our forces if the enemy utilized his full military potential.

POLICY NOT The tragedy is that since the advent
DEFINED of the war with Red China there has
been no definition of the political policy
which would provide a solution for the new problems
thereby created. This has resulted in a policy vacuum
heretofore unknown to war.

However great the effort to distract attention from the
main issues by introducing into public discussion extrane-
ous and irrelevant matters, the fundamental question still
remains the same—what is the policy for Korea?

Having aided through blundering diplomacy the
gaining of Communist control over China,

the failure to enunciate a simple forthright and positive statement of policy understandable to the world as firm assurance against any future trafficking with the Communist movement in Asia, arouses gravest doubts and fears.

DANGEROUS SHIFT IN CONCEPT Recent events point to a startling and dangerous shift in our basic military concept. After Communist China committed itself to war against our forces in Korea, our political and military leaders set aside our traditional military policy calling for the employment of all available power and means to achieve a prompt and decisive victory and adopted instead the doctrine of defense.

FAILURE INVITED Every distinguished military leader of the past and all military experience from the beginning of time warns this but invites failure. Under this new conception, novel indeed to the American military character, we are required in the midst of deadly war to soften our blows and send men into battle with neither promise nor hope of victory. We have deprived them of supporting military power already on hand and available which would blunt the enemy's blows against them, save countless American lives, fulfill our commitment to the tragic people of Korea and lead to the victorious end of a war which has already left so many thousands of American soldiers maimed or dead.

More than this, it could and would have removed the Chinese Communists as a threat to freedom in Asia and the peace of the world for generations to come.

In Korea, despite the magnificent performance of our fighting forces, the result has been indecisive. The high moral purpose which so animated and inspired the world yielded to the timidity and fear of our leaders as after defeating our original enemy a new one entered the field which they dared not fight to a decision.

APPEASEMENT ON BATTLEFIELD Appeasement thereafter became the policy of war on the battle-field. In the actual fighting with this new enemy we did not lose but neither did we win. Yet, it can be accepted as a basic principle proven and reproven since the beginning of time that a great nation which enters upon war and fails to see it through to victory must accept the full moral consequences of defeat.

I have believed a realistic policy should fill the long existing vacuum left in the wake of Red China's commitment to war against us—a policy designed to affect the early restoration of peace, through victory, with a consequent saving of countless American lives. It is difficult to ask men to fight and die unless we give them a realistic mission and means to accomplish it.

Could there be anything more discouraging and shocking to our soldiers on the line than the deprecating reference to their fierce and savage struggle as a "police action?" Could anything be more agonizing to the mothers of their dead than the belittling reference to it by the Joint Chiefs of Staff as the "Korean skirmish?" What a lack of perspective! What a failure to place first things first! What a complete callousness to human feeling and soldier dignity!

How fantastically unrealistic it is for them to refuse

to accept the factuality that we are already at war—a bitter, savage and costly war.

AVOIDANCE OF RESPONSIBILITY
If all other evidence were ignored, our mounting dead would alone stand as mute evidence that it is war in which we are now actually engaged. Yet, despite this, they seek to avoid the grave responsibility inherent in the fact of war; seek to divert public thought from the basic issue which war creates; how may victory be achieved with a minimum of human sacrifice. It is not a question of who wants war and who wants peace. All men of good conscience earnestly seek peace. The method alone is in issue. Some, with me, would achieve peace through a prompt and decisive victory at a saving of human life, others through appeasement and compromise of moral principle, with less regard for human life. The one course follows our great American tradition, the other but can lead to unending slaughter and our country's moral debasement.

The reason given for such a course has little validity. It has been argued in justification and seemingly to soothe the public concern that the application of conventional war measures against our enemy might provoke the Soviet into launching the Third World War.

> Yet, since the end of the Second World War, without committing a single soldier to battle, the Soviet, aided by our own political blunders, has gained a dominion over territory and peoples without parallel in all history—a dominion which it will take years for it to assimilate and administer.

What then would be its purpose in provoking a war of most doubtful result to the Communist cause? I have strong doubt that the start of a major war anywhere enters the Soviet plans at this stage. If and when it does, it will be at a time and place and under circumstances dictated with scarce regard to the incidents of Korea.

BLACKMAIL AND VIOLENCE   There are some who for varying reasons would appease Red China. They are blind to history's clear lesson. For history teaches with unmistakable emphasis that appeasement but begets new and bloodier war. It points to no single instance where the end has justified the means—where appeasement has led to more than a sham peace. Like blackmail, it lays the basis for new and successively greater demands, until, as in blackmail, violence becomes the only other alternative.

Why, my soldiers asked of me, surrender military advantages to an enemy in the field? I could not answer. Some may say to avoid spread of the conflict into an all-out war with China; others, to avoid Soviet intervention. Neither explanation seems realistic. China is already engaging with the maximum power it can commit and the Soviet will not necessarily mesh its actions with our moves. Like a cobra, any new enemy will more likely strike whenever it feels that the relativity in military or other potential is in its favor on a world-wide basis.

We have been told of the war in Korea that it is the wrong war, with the wrong enemy, at the wrong time and in the wrong place. Does this mean that they intend and indeed plan what they would call a right war, with a right enemy, at a right time and in the right place? If successful in mounting the North Atlantic Pact in 1953 or 1954 or at one of the ever changing dates fixed for its consummation, what comes then? Do we mean to throw down the gage of battle. Do we mean to continue the fantastic fiscal burden indefinitely to our inevitable exhaustion?

THE DOCTRINE OF PASSIVE DEFENSE In every war in which we have heretofore engaged, we have counter-balanced manpower with the doctrine of attack through our matchless scientific development. Yet, in Korea, we are admittedly applying the doctrine of passive defense which in all history has never won a war—a doctrine which has been responsible for more military disaster than all other reasons combined. Does experience teach us nothing? Has shifting expediency replaced logical reasoning?

DEATH RATHER THAN SLAVERY The tragedy of Korea is further heightened by the fact that as military action is confined to its territorial limits, it condemns that nation, which it is our purpose to save, to suffer the devastating impact of full naval and air bombardment, while the enemy's sanctuaries are fully protected from such attack and devastation. Of the nations of the world, Korea alone, up to now, is the sole one which has risked its all against Communism.

The magnificence of the courage and fortitude of the Korean people defies description. They have chosen to risk death rather than slavery.

As long as history is written, the shame of this will be recorded, but its more immediate consequences will be found in the loss of the faith of Asia in our nation's pledged word and the consequent undermining of the foundations to the future peace of the world.

For our failure to sustain our solemn commitments in Korea will probably mean the ultimate loss of all of continental Asia to international Communism.

DREAM OF CENTURIES It might well mean foreclosure upon the chances the Chinese may have had to throw off the chains of Red tyranny and oppression. It perhaps will even mean the ultimate fulfillment of the Russian dream of centuries to secure warm-water outlets to the south as a means of gaining a military posture of global omnipotence, with the hope of ultimate domination over the seaborne commerce of the world. Beyond Asia, Africa would then be exposed to Communist hordes dominating the Indian Ocean area, and Europe would come under a real threat of invasion. Prejudiced and willful voices scoffed at this warning, but there is where the Communists elected to challenge our spiritual and military strength and

there is where we have failed adequately to meet the challenge, even though we had the military resource and means at our command.

Our failure has been of the spirit, not of the arms—a bankruptcy of leadership in our American tradition. Yet this failure has furnished the Soviet the passkey to world conquest. Small wonder that such weakness and vacillation should cause us loss of faith and respect abroad. Not since the early days of the Republic has our nation been so reduced in the universal esteem. Never have we as a people been held in such doubt by others.

FUTILITY OF SACRIFICES Now that the fighting has temporarily abated the outstanding impression which emerges from the scene is the utter uselessness of the enormous sacrifice in life and limb which

has resulted. A million soldiers on both sides and unquestionably at least a like number of civilians are maimed or
dead. A nation has been gutted and we stand today just
where we stood before it all started. The threat of aggression upon the weak by these callously inclined among the
strong has not diminished. Indeed nothing has been set-
tled. No issue has been decided.

No words can excuse or relieve the enormous disaster
to the Korean people we are pledged to protect.

> The protection we offer these unfortunate people,
> indeed may well resolve itself into their complete
> obliteration. To what greater depths might morality
> possibly sink?

Mighty efforts are underway to conceal these facts. But
the march of events and the common sense of the American people cannot fail ultimately to reveal the full truth.

Two great questions about Korea still remain unan-
swered. First, why did they start the war if they did not
intend to win it? Second, what do they intend to do now
—go on piling up our dead indefinitely with no fixed purpose or end in sight?

Hardened old soldier though I am—my very soul re-
volts at such unnecessary slaughter.

Failure of Leadership

SIX YEARS AGO with a few strokes of the pen a calm descended upon the battlefields of the world and the guns grew silent. Military victory had been achieved for our cause and men turned their thoughts from the task of mass killing to the higher duty of international restoration, from destroying to rebuilding, from destruction to construction. Everywhere in the free world they lifted up their heads and hearts in thanksgiving for the advent of a peace in which ethics and morality, based upon truth and justice, might thereafter fashion the universal code.

Then more than ever in the history of the modern world, a materially strong and spiritually vibrant leadership was needed to consolidate the victory into a truly enduring peace for all of the human race. America, at the very apex of her military power, was the logical nation to which the world turned for such leadership.

It was a crucial moment—one of the greatest opportunities ever known. But our political and military leaders failed to comprehend it.

Sensitive only to the expediencies of the hour, they dissipated with reckless haste that predominant military power which was the key to the situation. Our forces were rapidly and completely demobilized and the great stores of war material which had been accumulated were disposed of with irresponsible waste and abandon.

The world was then left exposed and vulnerable to an international Communism whose long publicized plan had been to await just such a favorable opportunity to establish dominion over the free nations. The stage had perhaps been unwittingly set in secret and most unfortunate war conferences.

VICTORY FORFEITED   The events which followed will cast their shadow upon history for all time. Peoples with long traditions of human freedom progressively fell victims to a type of international brigandage and blackmail. The so-called "iron curtain" descended rapidly upon large parts of Europe and Asia. As events have unfolded, the truth has become clear.

Our great military victory has been offset, largely because of military unpreparedness, by the political successes of the Kremlin.

Our diplomatic blunders increased as our senseless disarmament became a reality. And now the disastrous cycle is completed as those same leaders who lost to the world the one great chance it has had for enduring universal peace, frantically endeavor, by arousing a frenzy of fear throughout the land, to gear anew our energies and resources, to rebuild our dissipated strength and to face again a future of total war.

Our need for adequate military defense, with world tensions as they were and are, is and should have been completely evident even before the end of the war.

By what faith then can we find hope in those whose past judgments so grievously erred—who deliberately disarmed in the face of threatening Communism? Can they now be blindly trusted as they so vehemently demand to set an unerring course to our future well-being and security?

SECURITY IN STRENGTH I recall so vividly the American Legion's warning to the country at the close of the war. Its resolution read as follows:

> "—the only present guarantee of our nation's safety and freedom and the best presently available assurance of world peace is to have in the hands of this great peace-loving nation the mightiest armament in the world."

This was sound and far-sighted advice which considered the present and drew upon the lessons and experience of the past. Had it been heeded by our political and military leaders, we would have been able to consolidate our great moral and military victory and lead the world to an enduring peace. We would not now be frantically endeavoring to restore our dissipated military strength. The Soviet would be but a negative influence upon world affairs and the earth would be a much gentler place on which to live. But our leaders failed to heed that advice.

> They failed to recognize the opportunity for leadership which victory had cast. They failed to see the enormity of the Communist threat to an impoverished postwar world.

FOREIGN INFLUENCES I have been amazed, and deeply concerned, since my return, to observe the extent to which the orientation of our national policy tends to depart from the traditional courage, vision and forthrightness which has animated and guided our great leaders of the past, to be now largely influenced, if not indeed in some instances dictated from abroad and dominated by fear of what others may think or others may do.

> Never before in our history can precedent be found for such a subordination of policy to the opinions of others with a minimum regard for the direction of our own national interest. Never before have we geared national policy to timidity and fear.

The guide, instead, has invariably been one of high moral principle and the courage to decide great issues on the spiritual level of what is right and what is wrong. Yet, in Korea today, we have reached that degree of moral trepidation that we pay tribute in the blood of our sons to the doubtful belief that the hand of a blustering potential enemy may in some way be thus stayed.

SEEDS OF WAR Munich, and many other historical examples, have taught us that diplomatic appeasement but sows the seeds of future conflict. Yet, oblivious to these bloody lessons, we now practice a new and yet more dangerous form of appeasement—appeasement on the battlefield whereunder we soften our blows, withhold our power, and surrender military advantages, in apparent hope that in some nebulous way by so doing a potential enemy will be coerced to desist from attacking us.

In justification for this extraordinary action it is pleaded by those responsible for the condition of our national defense that we are not prepared to fight. I cannot accept such an estimate. I believe that, much as we abhor war and should do anything honorable to avoid it, our country has the inherent strength to face and defeat any who may attack.

I should be recreant, moreover, to my obligations of citizenship did I fail to warn that the policies of appeasement on which we are now embarked carry within themselves the very incitation to war against us. If the Soviet does strike it will be because of the weakness we now display rather than the strength we of right should display.

RESPONSIBILITY CLEARLY PLACED If, however, we be so weak in fact that we must cower before the verbal brandishments of others, the responsibility for such weakness should be a matter of the gravest public concern.

Who, we should ask, is responsible for the reduction of our military strength from the greatest on earth at war's end to that they now estimate is inadequate even to support our moral commitments? Who plunged us into the Korean war and assumed other global commitments in the face of such alleged weakness, without reckoning and being ready to meet their potential consequence? Who is responsible for so grave a past failure which has brought our nation to so ignominious a pass that we must plead weakness before our fellow nations?

These are questions to which the nation should address itself, if it would be in a position to assess the policy judgment now in being and yet to be formulated. For it is elementary that if the defense of these policies is valid and we are indeed as weak as is pleaded, they who bear full responsibility for such weakness and they who formulate present policy are one and the same. Can we therefore accept their present and future judgments in the light of past failures without the most serious misgivings as to our future fate as a free and sovereign nation?

AMBITION AND GREED   The national administration has been and is under a control characterized by narrow vision and overriding personal ambition. The power of government was used as a political leverage to obtain more and greater centralization of authority. Political greed became the dominant factor in government and the fortunes of the political party of the administration began to receive primary consideration over and above the public interest.

Laws and clearly defined precedents which obstructed this concentration of power were brushed aside and the democracy of representative government began to yield to the concept of governmental autocracy. In the ensuing movement toward the ascendancy of men over laws, the meaning and intent of the Constitution became rapidly corrupted.

BEWILDERMENT AND CONFUSION   Propaganda was the mighty weapon through which control was sought. The people were first brought to a state of bewilderment and confusion through the agitation among the masses of fear and misunderstanding. Then followed a mighty effort to inject upon the American scene a system of mass thought control—a plan which failed of success only because of the rugged individualism still characteristic of the American people. Time and again in their innate wisdom they have sensed the tragic errors inherent in our misguided public policy. They have demanded changes, not only in policy, but in responsible appoIntive officials. But such demands have gone unheeded and men who have lost the public confidence have arbitrarily been protected in their exercise of the power of government.

Grievous, indeed, have been the blows at the very roots of the concept that government is "of the people, by the people and for the people."

THE REAL MENACE It is not from threat of external attack that we have reason for fear. It is from those insidious forces working from within. It is they that create the basis for fear by spreading false propaganda designed to destroy those moral precepts to which we have clung for direction since the immutable Declaration of Independence became the great charter of our liberty.

This campaign to pervert the truth and shape or confuse the public mind with its consequent weakening of moral courage is not chargeable entirely to Communists engaged in a centrally controlled world wide conspiracy to destroy all freedom. For they have many allies, here as elsewhere who, blind to reality, ardently support the general Communist aims while reacting violently to the mere suggestion that they do so.

THERE ARE THOSE There are those who subvert morality as the means to gain or entrench power. There are those who, believing themselves liberals, chart a course which can but lead to destruction. There are those cynically inclined whose restless impulse is ever seeking change. There are those who are constantly trying to alter our basic concepts of freedom and human rights. There are those who seek to prevent man from fearlessly speaking their minds according to the dictates of their conscience. There are those who plan to limit our individual right to share in the sovereign power of the people.

> There are those who seek to subvert government from being the guardian of the people's rights, to make of it an instrument of despotic power.

There are those who plan to alter the constitutional checks and balances established to preserve the integrity of our coordinate branches. There are those who seek to make the burden of taxation so great and the progressive increase so alarming that the spirit of adventure, tireless energy and masterful initiative which built the material strength of the nation shall become stultified and inert. There are those who seek to make all men servants of the State. There are those who seek to change our system of free enterprise which, whatever its faults, commands the maximum of energy and human resource and provides the maximum of benefits in human happiness and contentment.

Government has assumed progressively the arrogant mantle of oligarchic power, as the great moral and ethical principles upon which our nation grew strong have been discarded or remolded to serve narrow political purposes.

LIBERTY IN JEOPARDY Whether it be by accident or design, such policy, formulated with reckless indifference to the preservation of constitutional liberty and our free enterprise economy, coupled with the rapid centralization of power in the hands of a few, is leading us toward a Communist state with as dreadful certainty as though the leaders of the Kremlin themselves were charting our course. It implements the blueprints of Marx and Lenin with unerring accuracy and gives stark warning that, unless the American people stem the present threatening tide, human liberty will inevitably perish from our land.

THE IMMEDIATE MENACE What, I have been asked, is our greatest internal menace? If I were permitted but one sentence of reply, but one phrase of warning—it would be—

> "end invisible government based upon propaganda and restore truly representative government based upon truth."

For propaganda is the primary instrument of totalitarian rule, whether Communist or Fascist, and, incredible as it may seem to those of my generation, it is practiced as though it were a legitimate art or science. Suppress the truth, curtail free expression and you destroy the basis of all the freedoms.

We have indeed reached an astounding concept of morality when an official estimate such as that put out in December 1949 on Formosa, is now stated to be false and to have been intentionally publicized in order to mislead public opinion. Propaganda of this type closely parallels the Soviet system which we so bitterly condemn. Human liberty has never survived where such practice has flourished.

FEAR OF REPRISAL Indivisible from this trend and probably contributory to it, is a growing tendency to overlook certain forms of laxity in high quarters. Petty corruption in the public administration is a disease unfortunately common to all nations but I refer to an even more alarming situation. Men of significant stature in national affairs appear to cower before the threat of reprisal if the truth be expressed in criticism of those in higher public authority. For example, I find in existence a new and heretofore unknown and dangerous concept that the members of our armed forces owe primary allegiance and loyalty to those who temporarily exercise the authority of the executive branch of government, rather than to the country and its constitution which they are to defend.

No proposition could be more dangerous. None could cast greater doubt upon the integrity of the armed services. For its application would at once convert them from their traditional and constitutional role as the instrument for the defense of the Republic into something partaking of the nature of a pretorian guard owing sole allegiance to the political master of the hour.

While for the purpose of administration and command the armed services are within the executive branch of the government, they are accountable as well to the Congress, charged with the policy making responsibility, and to the people, ultimate repository of all national power. Yet so inordinate has been the application of the executive power that members of the armed services have been subjected to the most arbitrary and ruthless treatment for daring to speak the truth in accordance with conviction and conscience.

KEYSTONE DESTROYED   Truth has ceased to be the keystone to the arch of our national conscience and propaganda has replaced it as the rallying media for public support. Corruption and rumors of corruption have shaken the people's trust in the integrity of those administering the civil power.

I have faith that the American people will not be

fooled—that they will demand that the national policy be charted to a course of international realism without regard to domestic expediency—diplomacy rather than intrigue.

The potentiality of America's industrial strength in support of our expanding armament is guarantee against the wilfully designed military action against us.

> But wars can come about through blundering statesmanship animated by a lust for political power. Our course can and must be designed to promote the peace.

This can only be if we regain our moral balance and follow a course of international justice for all peoples, without taking sides in issues which are not directly our concern.

Other issues which deeply stir the conscience of the American people are many and varied, but all stem from irresponsibility in leadership. Domestic policy is largely dictated by the political expediencies of the moment. Foreign policy is as shifting as the sands before the winds and tides. Spendthriftness and waste have lost us our heritage of stability; weakness and vacillation, the moral leadership of the world.

Aid to Europe and—Taxes

AT THE BIRTH OF THE NATION, Washington counseled strongly against our entering upon entangling alliances abroad lest we find ourselves involved in Europe's wars. This was sound advice then, but has been necessarily outmoded by the progress of civilization. For with the development of means of rapid communication, existing gaps between the several continental land masses have been narrowed and ocean barriers in themselves no longer set the stage for continental isolation nor offer an assured degree of protection for continental shores. As a consequence, it is impossible to disassociate ourselves from the affairs of Europe and Asia. Major warfare in either has become our immediate military concern, lest they fall under the domination of those hostile to us and intent upon predatory incursions against our own land. To counteract the potentiality of this danger, we have acted both in the East and in the West.

POSITION IN THE PACIFIC Of direct and immediate bearing upon our national security are the changes wrought in the strategic potential of the Pacific Ocean in the course of the past year. Prior thereto, the western strategic frontier of the United States lay on the littoral line of the Americas with an exposed island salient extending out through Hawaii, Midway, and Guam to the Philippines. That salient proved not an outpost of strength but an avenue of weakness along which the enemy could and did attack. The Pacific was a potential area of advance for any predatory force intent upon striking at the bordering land areas.

All this was changed by our Pacific victory. Our strategic frontier then shifted to embrace the entire Pacific Ocean which became a vast moat to protect us as long as we did hold it. Indeed, it acts as a protective shield for all of the Americas and all free lands of the Pacific Ocean area. We control it to the shores of Asia by a chain of islands extending in an arc from the Aleutians to the Marianas held by us and our free allies. From this island chain we can dominate with sea and air power every Asiatic port from Vladivostok to Singapore and prevent any hostile movement into the Pacific.

COMMUNIST INTENTION Across the Atlantic we have no similar island defense chain; but in view of the openly flaunted intention of international Communism to destroy throughout the world the concept of freedom and bring peoples everywhere under the subjugation and terror of police rule, it has become necessary to help the free nations of Western Europe prepare against the threat of predatory attack by Communist forces now occupying Eastern Europe.

And generally throughout the world our policy has been enunciated to extend a helping hand to others whose freedom is threatened and who have the will but lack

the entire resource essential to their own defense. The
soundness of this concept will depend upon the wisdom
with which it is administered. Recklessly and abnormally
applied, it could encompass our own destruction. This
country obviously lacks the resource militarily to defend
the world. It has the resource, however, reasonably to
assist in that defense. But such assistance must be contributory to, rather than in place of maximum local national effort. It should be extended only upon condition:

> That assistance to others be really for defense and
> that it should be so limited as not to deplete our own
> resources to the point of imperiling the survival of
> our own liberties; and that those we would assist be
> animated by the same love of freedom as we, and
> possess the will and determination to pledge their
> own lives and full resource to secure their own
> defense.

**FALLACIOUS
THINKING** On the strict observance of these conditions rests our hope that present efforts
to bolster Western Europe may justify
the additional burden it places upon our own people.
There are, however, many disturbing signs and reports to
the contrary. There are many of the leaders and people
of Western Europe who mistakenly believe that we assist
them solely to protect ourselves, or to assure an alliance
with them should our country be attacked. This is indeed
fallacious thinking. Our potential in human and material
resource, in alignment with the rest of the Americas, is
adequate to defend this hemisphere against the threat
from any power or any association of powers.

We do desire to retain our traditional friends and
allies in Europe; but such an alliance must rest upon
spiritual bonds fabricated from a mutuality of pur-

pose and a common heritage of principle—not an alliance to be secured at a price.

SHARING OF WEALTH There are other disturbing signs that some of the peoples we seek to bolster are showing a lack of will to muster their own full resource in their own defense. There appear to be many among them who feel that their defense is and should be our sole responsibility and that beyond a token military collaboration they should confine their own energy and resource to the building of their civilian economy—some indeed who go so far as to advocate that money appropriated by our Congress for their military defense should be diverted to civilian purpose.

The startling thing is that such viewpoints are not lacking in support among our own leaders. Apparently some of them, more in line with Marxian philosophy than animated by a desire to preserve freedom, would finance the defense of others as a means of sharing with them our wealth.

This wealth, accumulated by our own initiative and industry under the incentives of free enterprise, would then serve as the means of covering socialist or communist deficits abroad. The ultimate effect, whatever the intent, would be to reduce our own standard of life to a level of universal mediocrity.

OUR COMMITMENT We have committed ourselves to contribute six ground divisions to Western Europe, notwithstanding that only a small fraction of the great masses of its peoples have been called to the colors. Indeed, if the human resource and industrial potential of the Western European nations were effectively employed for defense, there would be a minimum need for American ground forces or even great quantities of American munitions. Air and naval power, yes, but little honest necessity for ground troops—unless it be solely for morale purposes.

Actually if the European nations have the will to defend themselves, no question of morale would be involved. Our efforts to whip up enthusiasm among the Western European peoples for the defense of their own liberties finds neither precedent nor support in common sense or logic.

PLEASING TO SOVIET   One thing we must clearly understand is that the very course on which we are now embarked carries within itself grave risks to our own survival.

> The exhaustive effort to build our own military power and supplement that of other free nations, however justified, is probably more or less in accord with Soviet planning.

For just as we expend our resources to build military strength, inversely we progressively reduce ourselves to economic weakness, with a consequent growing vulnerability to the internal stresses and strains manipulated by Communists and their agents in our midst. It may indeed prove that the preparation for a war which may never occur will exhaust us materially as completely as would such a war itself.

> Our leaders must throw off the complacent belief that the only threat to our survival is from without. All freedoms lost since war's end have been the result of internal pressures rather than external assault.

CHANGE IN DESIGN   Our government now differs substantially from the design of our forefathers as laid down in the Constitution. They envisaged a federation of sovereign states with only such limited power resting in the federal authority as became necessary to serve the common interests of all. But under the stress of national emergencies during the past two decades, there has been a persistent and progressive centralization of power in the Federal Government with only superficial restoration to the States and the people as emergencies subsided.

This drift has resulted in an increasingly dangerous paternalistic relationship between Federal Government and private citizen, with the mushrooming of agency after agency designed to control the individual. Authority specifically reserved to the States by constitutional mandate has been ignored in the ravenous effort to further centralize the political power.

STATUS OF STATE DEPARTMENT Within the Federal Government itself there has been a further and dangerous centralization. For example, the Department of State, originally established for the sole purpose of the conduct of foreign diplomacy, has become in effect a general operating agency of government, exercising authority and influence over many facets of executive administration formerly reserved to the President or the heads of other departments. The Department of State indeed is rapidly assuming the character of a Prime Ministry, notwithstanding that its Secretary is an appointed official, neither chosen by nor answerable directly to the people.

FATAL DETOUR This drift toward totalitarian rule is reflected not only in this shift toward centralized power, but as well in the violent manner in which exception is taken to the citizen's voice when raised in criticism of those who exercise the political power. There seems to be a determination to suppress individual voice and opinion, which can only be regarded as symptomatic of the beginning of a general trend toward mass thought control. Abusive language and arbitrary action, rather than calm, dispassionate and just argument, ill becomes the leadership of a great nation conceived in liberty and dedicated to a course of morality and justice. These pressures have already caused us to depart sharply from the course so long held toward national strength and moral greatness.

> Our economic stature built under the incentives of free enterprise is imperiled by our drift through the back door of confiscatory taxation toward State Socialism.

INCENTIVES CURBED There has resulted an inevitable suppression of the incentive to maximize human energy, to encourage creative initiative, and to transform capital in one form to produce capital more needed in another. Our political stature built upon wise and self effacing statesmanship and sound domestic policy, has been sadly impaired by a succession of diplomatic blunders abroad and reckless spendthrift aims at home. Many peoples have lost faith in our leadership, and there is a growing anxiety in the American home as disclosures reveal graft and corruption over a broad front in our public service. Those charged with its stewardship seem either apathetic, indifferent or in seeming condonation.

Expenditure upon expenditure, extravagance upon extravagance have so burdened our people with taxation and fed the forces of inflation that our traditionally high standard of life has become largely fictitious and illusory. Apart from the direct income tax impounded at source, every necessity of life gives constant warning of the diminishing value of both national currency and private income.

FALSE SECURITY As always, it is the great masses of the people, not the rich or prosperous, but the farmer, the laborer, and the average office worker who suffer the most.

Some of these penalties are now obscured by the reckless extravagance of government spending which creates a false sense of security, but the day of reckoning is inevitable and understanding and fear of this injects a tragic apprehension in the American mind. Yet our leaders offer neither plan nor hope for a return to frugality and reason. Our remaining tax potential has been so depleted that, if the reckless policies of government continue unchecked, the direct confiscation of capital to meet the ensuing obligations is almost inevitable.

BLUEPRINT OF SOCIALISM Therein lies the blueprint to a Socialist State. Therein lies the great issue now before our people—shall we preserve our freedom, or yield it to a centralized government under the concept of Socialism. There can be no compromise. It must be all or nothing; the traditional American way of life, or a totalitarian concept imported from abroad. All other issues are but secondary to this one which strikes at the very roots of our personal liberties and representative form of government.

For Socialism, once a reality, destroys that moral fiber which is the creation of freedom. It breeds every device which produces totalitarian rule.

It is true that our Constitution established checks and balances designed to safeguard against such dangers, but such safeguard is ignored by those who seek to entrench personal political power through preferential treatment for some at the general expense of all. This carnival of special privilege cannot fail to undermine our heritage of character. It discourages development of those moral forces which would preserve inviolate our representative form of government, answerable to the free will of the electorate.

DESTRUCTIVE PATERNALISM   The great bulwark of the Republic, individual and collective self-reliance, is under constant threat through a carefully designed and progressive paternalism which renders both community and individual increasingly dependent upon the support of the Federal Government. In all areas of private welfare, the Socialist planners seek to inject the Federal hand to produce a progressive weakening of the structure of individual character.

The area of possible resistance to this creeping sabotage of freedom is being constantly narrowed as the Federal Government arrogates to itself more and more of the remaining tax potential. Should this trend continue, the Federal Government may well become for all practical purposes the sole taxing power. Thereafter the sovereignty of the States and autonomy of the communities, so pointedly recognized by the framers of the Constitution and nurtured through many generations of American life, will have been changed into a subservience to Federal direction in direct proportion to their dependence upon Federal grants for local support.

THE SAPPING PROCESS This process is sapping the initiative and energies of the people and leaves little incentive for the assumption of those risks which are inherent and unescapable in the forging of progress under the system of free enterprise. Worst of all, it is throwing its tentacles around the low income bracket sector of our society from whom is now exacted the major share of the cost of government. This renders its paper income largely illusory.

> The so-called "forgotten man" of the early thirties now is indeed no longer forgotten as the government levies upon his income as the main remaining source to defray reckless spendthrift policies.

More and more we work not for ourselves but for the State. In time, if permitted to continue, this trend cannot fail to be destructive. For no nation may survive in freedom once its people become the servants of the State, a condition to which we are now pointed with dreadful certainty.

> Labor, as always, will be the first to feel its frightful consequence.

It is quite true that some levy upon the people's earnings to pay the cost of government is unavoidable. But the costs of government, even discounting extraordinary military requirements, have risen to an accelerated, alarming and reckless rate. Nothing is heard from those in supreme executive authority concerning the possibility of a reduction or even limitation upon these mounting costs. No suggestion deals with the restoration of some semblance of a healthy balance. No plan is advanced for easing the crushing burden already resting upon the people. To the contrary, all that we hear are the plans by which such costs progressively may be increased. New means are constantly being devised for greater call upon the taxable potential.

ALTRUISM OR IMPRUDENCE We compound irresponsibility by seeking to share what liquid wealth we have with others. In so doing we recklessly speak of the billions we would set aside for the purpose, as though they were inconsequential. There can be no quarrel with altruism. Such has ever been a predominant quality making up the nobility of the American character.

> We should do all in our power to alleviate the suffering and hardship of other peoples, and to support their own maximum effort to preserve their freedom from the assaults of Communist imperialism.

But when this effort is carried beyond the ability to pay, or to the point that the attendant burden upon our own people becomes insufferable, or places our own way of life and freedom in jeopardy, then it ceases to be altruism and becomes reckless imprudence.

This nation's material wealth is built upon the vision and courage, the sweat and toil, hope and faith of our people. There has been no magic involved upon which we might again call to replenish our denuded coffers. We can either advance upon the security of sound principles or we can plunge on to the precipice of disaster toward which we are now headed in the dangerous illusion that our wealth is inexhaustible—and can therefore be limitlessly shared with others.

> It is argued that we must give boundlessly if we are to be assured allies in an emergency. I reject this

reasoning as an unwarranted calumny against well tested friends of long standing.

STRENGTH AND SURVIVAL   The survival of the free world is infinitely more dependent upon the maintenance of a strong, vigorous, healthy and independent America as a leavening influence than upon any financial aid which we might provide under our own existing stringencies.

The free world's one great hope for survival now rests upon the maintaining and preserving of our own strength. Continue to dissipate it and that one hope is dead.

GLOBAL THREAT   The Communist threat is a global one. Its successful advance in one sector threatens the destruction of every other sector. You cannot appease or otherwise surrender to Communism in Asia without simultaneously undermining our efforts to halt its advance in Europe. Yet the sad truth is that many in high authority show little interest in the Western Pacific area. And this despite our engagement in Korea in one of the most savage wars of American history, our long partnership with the Filipino people, our traditional ties of friendship with Asia, our alliance with New Japan and our Western Pacific defense frontier.

THE WILL TO BE FREE   The will to be free either exists in the human heart or all the money in the world cannot put it there. Thus, despite the billions we have poured abroad, I doubt that we have gained a single Communist convert to the cause of human freedom or inspired new or deeper friendships. And, as quite obviously the people of Western Europe do not generally share with our own leaders the fear of

Soviet military designs, despite these billions we seem to have made little progress in convincing them that they themselves should vigorously act to shore up their own defenses. We hear no clamor to pledge their own lives, their own fortunes and their own sacred honor in defense of their own liberties.

What gullibility to think the free world would fight for freedom in Europe after refusing to do so in Asia! As for me, I am as interested in saving Western Europe as any other threatened area, where the people show the will and the determination to mount their own full defensive power.

World War III

I AM NO SEER to predict whether or not the Soviet aims at ultimately provoking and engaging in a global struggle. I give him infinitely more credit, however, than to believe he would embark upon so reckless and ill-conceived a course. Up to now, there is no slightest doubt in my mind but that he has been engaging in the greatest bulldozing diplomacy history has ever recorded.

Without committing a single soldier to battle he has assumed direct or indirect control over a large part of the population of the world. His intrigue has found its success, not so much in his own military strength nor, indeed, in any overt threat of intent to commit it to battle, but in the moral weakness of the free world.

MORAL WEAKNESS It is a weakness which has caused many free nations to succumb to and embrace the false tenets of Communist propaganda. It is a weakness which has caused our own policy makers, after committing America's sons to battle, to leave them to the continuous slaughter of an indecisive campaign by imposing arbitrary restraints upon the support we might otherwise provide them through maximum employment of our scientific superiority, which alone offers hope of early victory. It is a weakness which now causes those in authority to strongly hint at a settlement of the Korean conflict, under conditions short of the objectives our soldiers were led to believe were theirs to attain and for which so many yielded their lives.

Of this we may be sure. The Soviet's moves, should it actually want war, will be dictated by its own assessment of the relativity of military force involved, actual and potential.

> It will not be so much influenced by the destruction it believes itself capable of inflicting upon us, as by the punishment it knows it itself would have to accept should it embark upon so reckless an adventure.

It will certainly not be influenced away from war by the blood tribute we are now paying in Korea to encourage it to preserve the peace.

ELEMENTARY LOGIC   This elementary logic, coupled with our own predominant superiority in many scientific facets of modern war, is ignored by those who seek support for our present unrealistic policies by the spread of a psychosis of fear throughout the land. They say that by meeting force with adequate counter-force in Asia we would expand the war and threaten the involvement of Europe, while painting a grim picture of the consequent devastation of our great cities. Nothing could be more unrealistic nor further from the truth. Our action would not be aimed at expanding but at ending the war and thus preventing its expansion. Our purpose would not be conquest but neutralizing such of the enemy's offensive power as is already hurled against us.

Europe's very survival is dependent upon our gaining a decisive victory in Asia where Communism has already thrown down the gage of battle.

MAJOR OPERATIONS ESSENTIAL   The existing policy of appeasement is defended on the ground that if our military reaction be conventional and we carry the war to the enemy in a manner calculated to destroy his capability of killing our sons and those whose protection we have assumed, we would incur the wrath of the Soviet and provoke the start of a world at war.

No argument could be more fallacious. The surest way to insure World War Three is to allow the Korean conflict to continue indecisively and indefinitely. The surest way, the only way, to prevent World War Three is to end the Korean conflict rapidly and decisively. Like a cancer, the only cure is by major operation.

Failure to take such decisive action—as in cancer—is but to invite infection of the entire blood stream. Yet the present plan of passive defense envisages the indefinite continuance of the indecisive stalemate with its compounding losses, in the vain hope that the enemy will ultimately tire and end his aggression. This, or that at some indefinite future date we will adopt the very policies of positive action designed to win the war and secure our stated objectives, which are now deprecated and decried.

CALLOUS AND UNREALISTIC   Could anything be more naïve, more unrealistic, more callous of our mounting dead? Could there be any greater inconsistency than the argument pursued that we can defeat Red China in Korea without risk of Soviet intervention but our attack upon its sustaining bases across the Yalu would render intervention inevitable?

> The defenders of the existing policy are the same who, suddenly and without slightest preparation or seeming consideration of the military and political potentialities, threw us into the conflict.

These are the very men who, in the face of mounting peril, deliberately demobilized us at the peak of our military strength, and then at the lowest point of our disarmament, with no slightest preparation or word of warning, plunged us into a war which they now seem afraid to win.

REASONS FOR RECALL   I hesitate to refer to my own relief from the Far Eastern Commands as I have never questioned the legal authority underlying such action. But the three sole reasons publicly stated by the highest authority clearly demonstrate the arbitrary nature of the decision.

The first reason given was that, contrary to existing policy, I warned of the strategic relationship of Formosa to American security and the dangers inherent in this area's falling under Communist control. Yet this viewpoint has since been declared by the Secretary of State, under oath before Congressional Committees, to have been and to be the invincible and long standing policy of the United States.

The second reason given was that I communicated my readiness to meet the enemy commander at any time to discuss acceptable terms of a cease fire arrangement. Yet, for this proposal, I was relieved of my command by the same authorities who since have received so enthusiastically the identical proposal when made by the Soviet Government.

The third and final reason advanced was my replying to a Congressman's request for information on the public subject then under open consideration by the Congress. Yet both Houses of Congress promptly passed a law confirming my action, which indeed had been entirely in accordance with a long existing and well recognized though unwritten policy. This law states that no member of the Armed Forces shall be restricted or prevented from communicating directly or indirectly with any member or members of Congress concerning any subject, unless such communication is in violation of law or the security and safety of the United States. And this formal enactment of basic public policy was approved without the slightest dissent of the President.

Is there wonder that men who seek an objective understanding of American policy thinking become completely frustrated and bewildered? Is there wonder that Soviet propaganda so completely dominates American foreign policy?

DIRECT AID TO RUSSIA   The issue of war or peace is not based upon any sudden and unexpected change in the course of world events, or even direction of Soviet policy. Long before even the Second World War, the Soviet was known to plan suppression of the concept of freedom and the advance of Communism throughout the world, as rapidly as conditions would permit.

We ourselves moulded these conditions to the Soviet's plan by providing extraordinary facility for it to so deploy its military forces as to permit direct and decisive pressure upon many of the free nations of Europe and Asia.

STAGE FOR WAR III The greatest hazard under which we now labor is the fear that the policy and propaganda of our present leadership may be setting the stage for a third world war. We are following the same path—the same historical record—the same political concept and leadership—which projected us into World War One, World War Two, and the war in Korea.

Since before the close of World War Two, this leadership has contributed to the building of Soviet military strength by extravagant lend-lease aid quite beyond any common military need; by acquiescing in Soviet troop concentration and dispositions at highly strategic points in Europe and Asia; by abandoning our war-time allies to the pressure of Soviet conquest; and, at the same time, divesting ourselves of our own vastly superior military strength, with reckless and precipitate haste. Against this background none will quarrel with the need to regain adequate security forces, not only that we may be prepared to meet any external threat, but that our diplomacy may be bulwarked with a power which will command universal respect.

But we cannot be satisfied with a leadership which declaims a devotion to peace with constant platitudinous statements and phrases while taking steps which inexorably tend to lead toward war.

FEAR OF HASTY ACTION We fear a repetition of such precipitate action as projected us into the Korean war with neither the advice nor consent of the Congress and in complete disregard of the carefully developed war policies and plans of the

United States. We deprecate a propaganda of fear among our people lest military levies and alliances be opposed by them. We question the hasty plunging into foreign quarrels, instead of holding the country on a high moral plane as an impartial and just arbiter of international dissensions. We dislike bombastic and provocative statements which settle nothing and but increase existing world tensions. We resent the docile acceptance of abusive pressure against us without the application of adequate counterpressure available to us.

PROVING GROUND FOR WAR   We cannot reconcile a declared purpose to defeat Communism while aligning our country with and supplying resources including arms to a Communist nation abroad and, at the same time, showing extraordinary reluctance to do the same for nations long recognized as uncompromising in their opposition to Communism. We condemn efforts to avoid possible public criticism by cloaking administrative functions behind a screen of secrecy under the doubtful pretext that the national security is directly involved.

We view with dismay the military advantage accorded the Soviet by permitting it long and protracted use of the Korean battle area as a training and proving ground for weapons and men with the protection of sanctuary beyond the Yalu.

We deplore the indefinite continuation of the Korean war when, ever since the entry of Communist China a year ago, we have had the means of bringing it to a prompt and victorious end and thus to save countless American lives and avoid the risk of its spreading into a global conflict inherent in its long continuance. And, in general, the pattern toward war is clearly defined. By confining their concern so assiduously to one area and ignoring the global nature of the Communist threat and the need to stop its predatory advance in other areas, they have become the "isolationists" of the present time.

> And it is a form of isolation which offers nothing but ultimate destruction. Our first line of defense for Western Europe is not the Elbe, it is not the Rhine— it is the Yalu. Lose there and you render useless the effort to implement the North Atlantic Pact or any other plan for regional defense.

NEW POLICY NEEDED The immediate problem calls for a dynamic political and military policy designed to secure the future and regain the lost faith of others in order that our moral influence may reassert itself to guide the world toward reason and right. We must rebuild the military power, wantonly dissipated despite warning and the clear portents of the situation in 1946, calmly and wisely and with sole regard to military requirements—not political expediency. We must not again permit our leaders to gamble with the national security to serve political ends.

We must rebuild our power not so much as a measure of defense against any imminently threatened attack, but as a means to regain the faith of those peoples of the world—traditional friends of our country—who now languish in the chains of Communist slavery or whose wills are controlled by Communist threat, treachery, coercion and brutality and to whom only the relativity of force longer has practical meaning.

Recently it was my valued privilege to address the American Legion assembled in annual national convention. To this gathering, in part, I said:

REARM WE MUST

"The American Legion, composed of men who know and detest war for the scourge that it is, is peculiarly well fitted to stand guard over our heritage of American liberty. It must exercise unrelaxed vigilance. It must ensure that neither political expediency nor foreign infatuation influences the expenditure of the vast sums now under contemplation for freedom's defense. It must exercise its great influence to the end that:

> we rearm—as rearm we must—in an atmosphere of confidence in our inherent strength, not under the hysteria of an artificially created fear;

that it is our implacable purpose to retain undisputed control of the seas, to secure undisputed control of the air, to vigorously implement our atomic program with a full commitment to the use as needed of the atomic weapon, and while maintaining a well-balanced and highly developed ground force, to charge to our allies the main responsibility for ground operations in defense of their own spheres of territorial interest; to curb the growing tendency of political and military leaders to publicize for political advantage classified data concerning scientific developments incident to our military effort, and thus to yield the all important element of surprise;

> to do all reasonably within our power to help preserve freedom for those who have the will and determination to do all in their power to defend their own freedom;

to avoid being drawn into unreasonable and unnecessary expenditures for armament to create an artificial domestic prosperity for political ends; to avoid contributing the fruits of our system of free enterprise to support Socialism or Communism abroad under the spurious pretense that it serves our own military security; to avoid aligning ourselves with colonial policies in Asia and the Middle East, lest we invite the enmity of the traditionally friendly peoples of those vast areas of the world; to give primary concern to our own security and the well being of our own people;

> to avoid distributing our wealth for the purpose of buying the loyalty of others, or of sharing with others the wealth and security which we hold in sacred trust for our progeny;

to apply all possible pressure, short of war, upon the Soviet or any associated power which by abuse and pressure upon us forces the expenditure of such vast outlays of our energy and resources as a measure of self-preservation; to avoid a protracted and indecisive war in Korea with its endless slaughter—the Chief of Staff of the Army recently testified before a Congressional Committee that it might last for ten years; to regain military faith in ourselves and the policies upon which our victories in past have always rested; to do all reasonably within our power to assist the Filipino and Japanese people to advance and fortify their liberties and the Chinese people to regain theirs; and, above all else,

> to preserve inviolate those great principles and ideals of moral authority upon which is based the American way of life and the nobility of the cause for which our soldiers fight."

NO SUBSTITUTE FOR VICTORY And in the formulation of such policies, it is well that we understand that battles are not won by arms alone. There must exist above all else a spiritual impulse

—a will to victory. This can only be if the soldier feels his sacrifice is to preserve the highest moral values. And we should understand that once war is forced upon us, there is no other alternative than to apply every available means to bring it to a swift end.

War's very objective is victory—not prolonged indecision. In war, indeed, there can be no substitute for victory.

CHAPTER EIGHT

Decision of the People

T HE COMPLEXITY brought about by dislocations in the wake of two world wars has caught our beloved country in the vortex of a confused, distressed and frightened world.

At war's end the main agency for maintaining the peace became the United Nations. This organization was conceived in a common desire that the scourge of war should not again be visited upon the earth. It was dedicated to the principle that all mankind of unalienable right should live in justice and liberty and peace.

> It represents perhaps the noblest effort man has yet made to evolve a universal code based upon the highest of moral precepts. It became the keystone to an arch of universal hope.

Yet in practice its efforts became increasingly doubtful of ultimate success. Its organization is inherently weak, legislatively, judicially and executively. It lacks legislative strength because its members, not being elected but merely appointed, are not answerable directly to the people. It lacks judicial strength because there is no accepted international code of sufficient moral authority or purpose to mould and guide its decisions. It lacks executive strength because it controls no agencies of sufficient power to enforce its mandates.

FAILURE APPARENT It threatens to fail—if the innate selfishness of its members does not yield to universal needs; if the mechanics of its operations are not corrected to prevent the will of one nation from counterbalancing the collective will of the others; if it does not obtain acceptance by member nations of its lawful decisions; if it does not stop obstructionist tactics, even by expulsion if necessary, of its own unruly members; if regional military alliances must be organized within its membership to undertake collective security measures against threat from other members; if it allows itself to be reduced to a mere forum for meaningless and acrimonious debate, and a springboard for propaganda.

Unless a strong and dynamic sense of responsibility emerges within its ranks capable of rallying the forces of good throughout the world; of establishing a higher moral tone to its deliberations and activities; of correcting its existing institutional and mechanical weaknesses, the United Nations may well go the way of its predecessor League and perish as a force to guide civilization.

THE VITAL TASK But the great moral and spiritual purpose which animated its formation—the abolition of war from the face of the earth—will always live and a way must be found to achieve that purpose.

This way cannot be found, however, if nations are so blind as not to see their own weaknesses—so weak as not to correct them.

We must lead the world down this road, however long

and tortuous and illusory it may now appear. Such is the role as I see it for which this great nation of ours is now cast. In this we follow the Cross. If we meet the challenge we cannot fail. On this problem of greatest universal concern, unless we address ourselves to the fundamentals we shall get no farther than the preceding generations which have tried and failed. Convention after convention has been entered into designed to humanize war and bring it under the control of rules dictated by the highest human ideals. Yet each war becomes increasingly savage as the means for mass killing are further developed.

WAR UNCONTROLLABLE You cannot control war; you can only abolish it. Those who shrug this off as idealistic are the real enemies of peace—the real war mongers. Those who lack the enterprise, vision and courage to try a new approach when none others have succeeded fail completely the most simple test of leadership.

Let us regain some of the courage and faith of the architects who charted the course to our past greatness. Let us look up as befits the most powerful nation on earth, both spiritually and physically.

> Let us tell all that while firmly and invincibly dedicated to the course of peace, we will not shrink from defending ourselves if the alternative is slavery or some other form of moral degradation.

Let us proudly reassume our traditional role of readiness to meet and vanquish the forces of evil at any time and any place they are hurled against us. Let us make clear our eagerness to abolish the scourge of war from the face of the earth just as soon as others are willing to rise to so

noble a stature with us. Let us renew our reverence for
the blood of our sons and strike with all the power we can
mount to support and protect those who now fight our
battles in distant lands. And above all else let us regain
our faith in ourselves and rededicate all that is within us
to the repair and preservation of our own free institutions
and the advance of our own free destiny.

PEOPLE   As I have traveled through the country
AWAKENING   since my return, I find a great transfor-
mation in American thought to be tak-
ing place. Our apathy is disappearing. American public
opinion is beginning to exert its immense power. The
American people are expressing themselves with dynamic
force on foreign policy.

This is exerting a profound influence upon the Soviet
course of action.

Few events in the life of our Republic have been of
more significant importance nor more heartening than
this rallying of the collective will of the American people.
They are putting pressure upon their own leaders and
upon the leaders of those with whom we are directly or
indirectly engaged. And just as it has cast its influence
upon policy and events abroad, it can be brought to bear
with no less telling effect upon policy and events at home.
Therein lies our best hope in the battle to save America—
the full weight of an aroused, informed and militant public opinion. To my fellow Americans I have said:

IN BOSTON   "To this section of the country men point
as the cradle of our freedom. For here
was established more than three centuries ago a declara-

tion of rights from which ultimately came the constitutional mandate guaranteeing our civil liberties. Here men arose militantly in protest against the tyranny of oppressive rule of burdensome taxation. Here men engaged in formal combat to sever the distasteful bonds of colonial rule. Here men etched the patriot's pattern which all races who harbored in their hearts a love for freedom have since sought to emulate. Here men, by their courage, vision and faith, forged a new concept of civilization."

IN SEATTLE "I have just crossed the continent in hours, where it took those who first pioneered the way as many long, tortuous and perilous months. Seattle proudly and majestically stands today at one hundred years of age full beneficiary of what the pioneering spirit has wrought upon this continent. It marks the fruition of the dream to bring the fruits of civilization to a vast and then uncharted wilderness. It has become a heritage which all Americans may share with pride and hope. The inspiration to be drawn from its one hundred years of the past builds faith in the next hundred years of the future.

"Many pessimistic voices are being raised today throughout the land. But the times are full of hope if the vision and courage and faith of the early pioneer continue to animate the American people in the discharge of their sovereign responsibilities.

The people have it in their hands to restore morality, wisdom and vision to the direction of our foreign and domestic affairs and regain the religious base which in times past assured general integrity in public and private life.

"Despite failures in leadership, they have it in their

power to rise to that stature which befits their lofty heritage of spiritual and material strength;

> to reject the Socialist policies covertly and by devious means being forced upon us; to stamp out Communist influence which has played so ill-famed a part in the past misdirection of our public administration;

to reorganize our government under a leadership invincibly obedient to our Constitutional mandates; to re-enforce existing safeguards to our economy of free enterprise; to reassert full protection for freedom of speech and expression and those other freedoms now threatened; to regain State and community autonomy; to renounce undue alien interference in the shaping of American public policy; and to re-establish our governmental process upon a foundation of faith in our American institutions, American traditions and the time-tested adequacy of American vision."

IN CLEVELAND "No section of our country symbolizes more forcefully the pattern of our National progress than does this great Midwest whose fertile fields and thriving industry combine to reflect the constructive energy of our people. You have moulded a standard and pattern of life known to no other nation of the world, and I pray that we will have the vision and courage and statesmanship to keep it that way—that we will preserve an America which will provide increasing, not diminishing, opportunities for human advancement."

IN TEXAS "Texas is a shining example of the power generated under conditions of human liberty. For in Texas men, given freedom of opportunity, have harnessed many of nature's vast stores and turned

the resulting energy and material resource into the building of a mighty nation dedicated to the advance of personal liberty and individual dignity. Nowhere are men
found more devoted to the concepts of freedom and the
preservation of the American system based upon truth
and justice. None have contributed more to the advance
of the traditional American ideal. None give more hope
that an America conceived in liberty will survive in liberty.

"Yet, if this is to be so, every American must firmly
share the responsibility attendant upon citizenship in a
republic. All must rally to the demand that administration of the civil power be on a level of morality which will
command the public confidence and faith; that truth re-
place false and slanted propaganda in public information; that cynicism give way to confidence that our course
of right will prevail; that fear and timidity be repudiated
as having no place in shaping our destiny; and that national policy be determined with primary regard to the
ultimate well-being of our own people.

"I have found here a vast reservoir of spiritual and
material strength which fills me with a sense of confidence
in the future of our nation. It confirms my faith that with
such resources none can excel us in peaceful progress nor
safely challenge us to the tragedy of war. These facts
should be thoroughly understood by every American citizen to offset efforts which are being made through propaganda to sow the seeds of fear and timidity in the American mind—to portray our nation as weak and our
potential enemies as strong. There could be no greater
disservice to our beloved country than is reflected in such
a fantastic effort to lower our own self-assurance and enhance that of those unfriendly to us."

IN MISSISSIPPI "As I stand before you and recall the South's mighty contribution to our beloved country, my heart is filled with pride that I, too, by right of birth may claim its great and noble traditions as my traditions, its lofty heritage of honor as my heritage. For when the past decade is adjudged by the historian of the future, he will surely record that in the forefront of the fight to preserve constitutional liberty to our country was the moral courage, the indomitable will and the broad vision of most of the statesmen of the South. It is they who stood guard in our hour of gravest peril. It is they who, departing from the tradition of politics, rose to magnificent heights of patriotism to challenge those forces which sought to impose upon the States the autocracy of centralized government."

ISSUES CLEARLY DEFINED The issues which today confront the nation are clearly defined and so fundamental as to directly involve the very survival of the Republic.

Are we going to preserve the religious base to our origin, our growth and our progress or yield to the devious assaults of atheistic or other anti-religious forces?

Are we going to maintain our present course toward State Socialism with Communism just beyond or reverse the present trend and regain our hold upon our heritage of liberty and freedom?

Are we going to squander our limited resources to the point of our own inevitable exhaustion or adopt commonsense policies of frugality which will insure financial stability in our time and a worth-while heritage in that of our progeny?

Are we going to continue to yield personal liberties and

community autonomy to the steady and inexplorable centralization of all political power or restore the Republic to constitutional direction, regain our personal liberties and reassume the individual State's primary responsibility and authority in the conduct of local affairs?

Are we going to permit a continuing decline in public and private morality or re-establish high ethical standards as the means of regaining a diminishing faith in the integrity of our public and private institutions?

Are we going to continue to permit the pressure of alien doctrines to strongly influence the orientation of foreign and domestic policy or regain trust in our own traditions, experience and free institutions and the wisdom of our own people?

In short, is American life of the future to be characterized by freedom or by servitude, strength or weakness. The answer must be clear and unequivocal if we are to avoid the pitfalls toward which we are now heading with such certainty. In many respects it is not to be found in any dogma of political philosophy but in those immutable precepts which underly the Ten Commandments.

CROSSROAD OF HISTORY We stand today at a critical moment of history—at a vital crossroad. In one direction is the path of courageous patriots seeking in humility but the opportunity to serve their country; the other that of those selfishly seeking to entrench autocratic power. The one group stands for implacable resistance against Communism; the other for compromising with Communism. The one stands for our traditional system of government and freedom; the other for a Socialist State and slavery. The one boldly speaks the truth; the other spreads propaganda, fear and deception. The one denounces excessive taxation, bureaucratic government and corruption; the other seeks more taxes, more bureaucratic power, and shields corruption.

> The people, as the ultimate rulers, must choose the course our nation shall follow. On their decision rests the future of our free civilization and the survival of our Christian faith.

Not for a moment do I doubt the decision or that it will guide the nation to a new and fuller greatness.

IN THE FACES OF THE PEOPLE Since my return, I have been encouraged to believe that our citizens will not complacently tolerate further incursions against their cherished liberties, and will move to correct this drift away from truly representative government. I have found this encouragement in the rare opportunity to search the faces of millions of my fellow countrymen. Therein I have been given understanding of the meaning of Abraham Lincoln when he said:

> ". . . to the salvation of the Union there needs but one single thing—the hearts of a people like yours. When the people rise in a mass, in behalf of the liberties of the country, truly it may be said that nothing can prevail against them. . . ."

I have seen in the faces of the American people that to which Mr. Lincoln prophetically referred. I have clearly seen that the soul of liberty is still living and vibrant in the American heart. It is neither Democratic nor Republican but American. It will assert itself by Constitutional process and with invincible force in the battle to save the Republic.

The people will still rule.

The MacArthurs in their native land — America.
ARTHUR — DOUGLAS — JEAN FAIRCLOTH MACARTHUR.

THE VACANT CHAIR

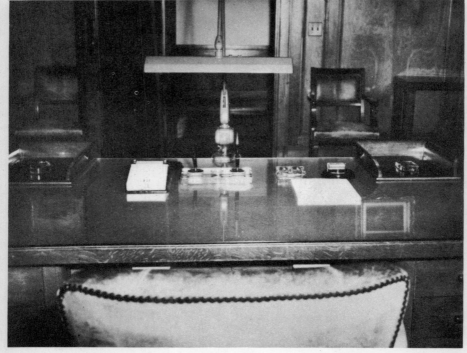

On April 12, 1951, General Douglas MacArthur, for the last time, visited his office in the Dai Ichi Building, Tokyo, which he had occupied for five years. General MacArthur's office, desk, and the chair left vacant as he departed.

GRIEF

Japanese in the multitude that lined the route to the Tokyo airport, silent and saddened, as General MacArthur boarded his plane for return to the United States.

On his arrival in San Francisco on April 16, 1951, tens of thousands of Californians flock to the Civic Center and the City Hall steps to hear General of the Army Douglas MacArthur express his pleasure at being once more in his native land and to say "God bless America."

INS Photo from Helicopter

A tumultuous throng of wildly cheering Californians crowds into the right of way as General MacArthur's car slowly threads its way to the San Francisco airport for the flight to Washington, D.C.

Members of the Senate and the House of Representatives give General Douglas MacArthur a standing ovation as he arrives to deliver his address before a joint session of the Congress.

Millions of people, silent and prayerful, gathered before tens of thousands of radios and televisions to listen to and witness the dramatic presentation of General MacArthur's message of dauntless courage and of faith. (*Upper*) Crowds jam-packed before television in smoking room of the Grain Exchange, Chicago. (*Lower*) Rapt listeners and watchers on a street gazing at television through a shopwindow.

Other men in other towns before other windows stopped to watch and wonder and crowds of women regained faith and hope while listening to General MacArthur's restatement of age-old truths.

From Washington across the nation, to the most remote towns and hamlets, Americans listened with bated breath and with misty eyes to General MacArthur saying, "I have just left your fighting sons in Korea. They have met all tests there and I can report to you they are splendid in every way. It was my constant effort to preserve them and end this savage conflict honorably and with the least loss of time and a minimum sacrifice of life." Not since Gettysburg had a man spoken with such feeling and such authority.

Down Pennsylvania Avenue a motorcycle escort led the motorcade that carried General MacArthur to the ceremonies on the grounds of the Washington Monument.

Acme Photo

Five hundred thousand people gather at the foot of the Washington Monument to hear General MacArthur restate, in clear and understandable terms, the great basic American principles.

Chicago Tribune Photo

On April 20, New York City staged its greatest parade. More than seven million people lined the ... of the ... which proceeded under a veritable curtain of ticker tape and confetti.

INS News Photo

A gathering of hundreds of thousands in City Hall Plaza. Amid the acclaim of a multitude, the mayor of New York presented General MacArthur with a special gold medal in recognition of the "city's esteem and affection" and for his uncompromising and dauntless "defense of human liberties."

On April 26, General MacArthur dedicated the State Street Bridge, Chicago, to the Heroes of Corregidor.

More than one million people in State Street roared approval when General MacArthur pledged, "I shall dedicate all of my energies to regaining that moral base which will restore the people's faith."

Acme Photo

General MacArthur traveled northward. Tens of thousands of people along the highway greeted him. In Waukegan, Illinois (*above*), more than one hundred thousand gathered to give tangible evidence of support to the vital message he enunciated.

Acme Photo

On April 27, General MacArthur officiated at the dedication of MacArthur Square in downtown Milwaukee. More than one million eager, cheering people were on hand. Hundreds of thousands with rapt attention heard him say: "It stands as solemn warning to those who would destroy freedom, either externally or internally. America will not now nor in the future yield that for which so many have died . . . It will serve to rally all Americans to the task of maintaining the moral strength which has built our past."

To the largest and most enthusiastic crowd ever assembled in Austin for a similar purpose, General MacArthur spoke before the legislature of Texas from the Capitol steps.

INP Sound Photo

In Dallas a wildly cheering multitude of Texans hail General MacArthur for his belief in our strength and his plea for a return to the concepts and principles of our forefathers.

Acme Photo

(*Upper*) In Houston, Texas, enthusiasm was unrestrained as General MacArthur's motorcade neared the center of this fastest-growing Southern metropolis.

(*Lower*) In Fort Worth tens of thousands of eager, vital Texans vie with other Texas cities in extending the utmost in Southern hospitality and approval.